SCHOLASTIC

100 MATHS LESSONS

Recommended system requirements:

- Windows: XP (Service Pack 3), Vista (Service Pack 2) or Windows 7 with 2.33GHz processor
- Mac: OS 10.6 to 10.8 with Intel Core™ Duo processor
- 1GB RAM (recommended)
- 1024 x 768 Screen resolution
- CD-ROM drive (24x speed recommended)
- 16-bit sound card
- Microsoft Word

For all technical support queries, please phone Scholastic Customer Services on 0845 6039091.

SCHOLASTIC

Book End, Range Road, Witney, Oxfordshire, OX29 0YD

www.scholastic.co.uk

© 2013, Scholastic Ltd

1 2 3 4 5 6 7 8 9   3 4 5 6 7 8 9 0 1 2

British Library Cataloguing-in-Publication Data
A catalogue record for this book is available from the British Library.

ISBN 978-1407-12840-5
Printed by Bell & Bain Ltd, Glasgow

Due to the nature of the web we cannot guarantee the content or links of any site mentioned. We strongly recommend that teachers check websites before using them in the classroom.

Contributor
Catherine Baker

Editorial team
Rachel Morgan, Emily Jefferson and Jenny Wilcox

Cover Design
Andrea Lewis

Design Team
Sarah Garbett, Shelley Best and Andrea Lewis

Contents

Introduction

This planning guide is designed to help support schools, subject coordinators and teachers to navigate the 2014 *National Curriculum in England* and to plan their school curriculum appropriately. It is now a requirement for all schools to publish their school curriculum online, and this handy planning guide can assist you with this task for this new curriculum.

The curriculum documentation for mathematics provides a yearly programme of study for Year 1 to Year 6. It can be a complex task to ensure that a progressive and appropriate curriculum is followed in all year groups. This planning guide aims to support you in this challenge.

The new curriculum has a much greater focus on varied and frequent practice of the fundamentals of mathematics – including addition and subtraction facts, multiplication and division tables. However, the intention of the curriculum is that pupils will also be able to use and apply this knowledge in solving problems by reasoning mathematically.

Reasoning mathematically and solving problems are requirements of the new curriculum: there are learning objectives that involve 'solving number problems and practical problems', 'solving multi-step problems', 'missing number problems' and 'measure and money problems'. The main coverage of using and applying mathematics, however, can be found in the aims of the curriculum:

> *The National Curriculum for mathematics aims to ensure that all pupils:*
> - *become **fluent** in the fundamentals of mathematics, including through varied and frequent practice with increasingly complex problems over time, so that pupils have conceptual understanding and are able to recall and apply their knowledge rapidly and accurately to problems*
> - ***reason mathematically** by following a line of enquiry, conjecturing relationships and generalisations, and developing an argument, justification or proof using mathematical language*
> - *can **solve problems** by applying their mathematics to a variety of routine and non-routine problems with increasing sophistication, including breaking down problems into a series of simpler steps and persevering in seeking solutions.*

Terminology

The curriculum terminology has changed; the main terms used are:

- **Domains:** the area of the subject, for mathematics the domains are 'Number and place value', 'Addition and subtraction' and so on.
- **Curriculum objectives:** by the end of Key Stage 1 and Key Stage 2, pupils are expected to know, apply and understand the matters, skills and processes detailed in the relevant programme of study.

About the book

The book provides content for each year group (Years 1–6) and includes:

- **Long-term planning:** The overview of the domains and what should be covered in that year. These are based upon the non-statutory guidance from the curriculum.

- **Progression:** This provides a year-by-year overview of how the children progress through the domains. The progression overview includes what children should already know from the previous year, what's covered in the current year and how this progresses into the following year.

- **Medium-term planning:** Six half-termly grids are provided for each year group. Each contains an overview of each week's planning including the topic being covered, the outcomes for that week and the learning objectives covered. Please note that due to space some of the curriculum objectives have been abbreviated. We recommend that you always refer to the full curriculum documentation in conjunction with the planning guide.

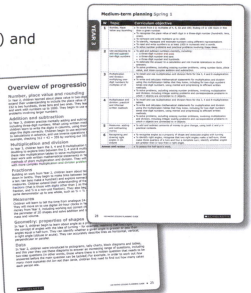

- **Background knowledge:** This explains key concepts relevant to the Year group to help support teacher's knowledge with the more technical curriculum coverage of mathematics.

The final four pages of the book support planning for mixed-aged classes by providing an overview of progression for Years 1–2, Years 3–4 and Years 5–6.

About the CD-ROM

The CD-ROM provides the long-term planning, progression, medium-term planning and background knowledge as editable Word files. These can be used and adapted to meet the needs of your school.

There is a simple menu screen on the CD-ROM. Simply navigate to the year group you require and then click on the button to open the associated file.

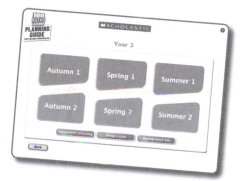

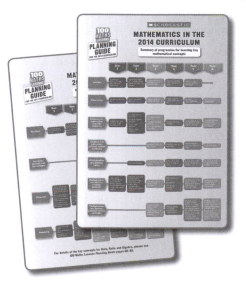

About the poster

The poster summarises the progression of key concepts in the mathematics National Curriculum. Display it in a central location, such as the staffroom, to help improve understanding of the new curriculum within your school.

Year 1 Long-term planning

Number and place value

• Children should practise counting (1, 2, 3), ordering (first, second, third), or to indicate a quantity (3 apples, 2 centimetres), including solving simple concrete problems, until they are fluent.

• They should begin to recognise place value in numbers beyond 20 by reading, writing, counting and comparing numbers up to 100, supported by concrete objects and pictorial representations.

• They should practise counting as reciting numbers and counting as enumerating objects, and counting in ones, twos, fives and tens from different multiples to develop their recognition of patterns in the number system (odd and even numbers). They connect these patterns with objects and with shapes, including through varied and frequent practice of increasingly complex questions.

• They recognise and create repeating patterns with objects and with shapes.

Multiplication and division

• Through grouping and sharing small quantities, children should begin to understand: multiplication and division; doubling numbers and quantities; and finding simple fractions of objects, numbers and quantities.

• They should make connections between arrays, number patterns, and counting in twos, fives and tens.

Measurement

• The pairs of terms mass and weight, volume and capacity, are used interchangeably at this stage.

• Children should move from using and comparing different types of quantities and measures using non-standard units, including discrete (e.g. counting) and continuous (e.g. liquid) measures, to using manageable common standard units.

• In order to become familiar with standard measures, children begin to use measuring tools such as a ruler, weighing scales and containers.

• Children should use the language of time, including telling the time throughout the day, first using o'clock and then half past.

Addition and subtraction

• Children should memorise and reason with number bonds to 10 and 20 in several forms (9 + 7 = 16; 16 – 7 = 9; 7 = 16 – 9). They should realise the effect of adding or subtracting zero. This establishes addition and subtraction as related operations.

• Children should combine and increase numbers, counting forwards and backwards.

• They should discuss and solve problems in familiar practical contexts, including using quantities. Problems should include the terms put together, add, altogether, total, take away, distance between, more than and less than, so that pupils develop the concept of addition and subtraction and are enabled to use these operations flexibly.

Fractions

• Children should be taught half and quarter as 'fractions of' discrete and continuous quantities by solving problems using shapes, objects and quantities. For example, they could recognise and find half a length, quantity, set of objects or shape. Children connect halves and quarters to the equal sharing and grouping of sets of objects and to measures, as well as recognising and combining halves and quarters as parts of a whole.

Geometry: position and direction

• Children should use the language of position, direction and motion, including: left and right, top, middle and bottom, on top of, in front of, above, between, around, near, close and far, up and down, forwards and backwards, inside and outside.

• Children should make half, quarter and three-quarter turns and routinely make these turns in a clockwise direction.

Geometry: properties of shapes

• Children should handle common 2D and 3D shapes, naming these and related everyday objects fluently. They should recognise these shapes in different orientations and sizes, and know that rectangles, triangles, cuboids and pyramids can be different shapes.

■ SCHOLASTIC

Overview of progression in Year 1

Number and place value

During the Foundation Stage, children counted and estimated groups of up to 10 objects. In Year 1, children extend their use of counting numbers to at least 100. They develop recognition of patterns in the number system (including odd and even numbers) by counting in ones, twos, fives and tens. Children use first, second, third for example when ordering items.

Children do not need to recognise the place value of each digit in a two-digit number as they will do this in Year 2. However, they should understand that they can tell whether a number is larger than another by looking at the first digit as well as the second digit.

Addition and subtraction

During the Foundation Stage, children related addition to combining two groups and subtraction to *taking away* when doing practical activities. In Year 1, children use mathematical statements to record addition and subtraction. They read, interpret and write the symbols +, − and =.

Through practice of addition and subtraction, children learn the number trios for numbers to 20 (8 + 5 = 13, 13 − 8 = 5, 13 − 5 = 8). They use different strategies to help them derive number facts, such as adding numbers in any order, or finding a difference by counting up.

Multiplication and division

In Year 1, children are introduced to the concepts of multiplication and division, although they will not use the standard signs (× and ÷) until Year 2. In practical activities, using arrays and physical objects such as blocks, children solve multiplication and division problems using small quantities. With support, children investigate the links between arrays, number patterns and their experience of counting in twos, fives and tens.

Fractions

Children learn to identify halves and quarters by solving practical problems – for example, finding half of a set of ten blocks or a quarter of a square. They learn that the concepts of a half and a quarter apply to objects and quantities as well as to shapes. They link the idea of halves and quarters back to the concepts of sharing and grouping, which they use in their work on multiplication and division. They will build on this in Year 2 when they learn to write simple fractions.

Measurement

In Year 1, children begin to use some common standard units, including measuring objects using rulers, weighing scales and jugs. They accurately use comparative language for length, weight, volume and time, such as longer/shorter, heavier than/lighter than, more/less, and quicker/slower.

Children read the time on analogue clocks to the hour and half-hour, and they learn to recognise different coins and notes. In Year 2, children will use standard units more independently and gain experience in telling the time and doing simple calculations with money.

Geometry: properties of shapes

In Year 1, children become familiar with a range of common 2D and 3D shapes, including rectangles, circles and triangles, cuboids, pyramids and spheres. They recognise these shapes in different orientations, sizes and contexts.

Geometry: position and direction

Children continue to use positional language accurately when describing where people or objects are in the environment. They experience the differences between half, quarter and three-quarter turns by practising making these turns in a clockwise direction.

Medium-term planning Autumn 1

W	Topic	Curriculum objective
1	Counting	• To count to and across 100, forwards and backwards, beginning with 0 or 1, or from any given number. • To identify and represent numbers using objects and pictorial representations including the number line, and use the language of: equal to, more than, less than (fewer), most, least.
2	Addition and subtraction to 5 or more (part 1)	• To read and write numbers from 1 to 20 in numerals and words. • When given a number, identify one more and one less. • To read, write and interpret mathematical statements involving addition (+), subtraction (−) and equals (=) signs. • To add and subtract one-digit and two-digit numbers to 20, including zero.
3	Addition and subtraction to 5 or more (part 2)	• To add and subtract one-digit and two-digit numbers to 20, including zero. • To solve simple one-step problems that involve addition and subtraction, using concrete objects and pictorial representations, and missing number problems.
4	Addition totals to 10	• To read, write and interpret mathematical statements involving addition (+), subtraction (−) and equals (=) signs. • To represent and use number bonds and related subtraction facts within 20. • To add and subtract one-digit and two-digit numbers to 20 (9 + 9, 18 − 9), including zero.

5	Properties of shape	• To recognise and name common 2D and 3D shapes, including:
		  • 2D shapes (rectangles (including squares), circles and triangles)
		  • 3D shapes (cuboids (including cubes), pyramids and spheres).

6	Addition and subtraction to 10	• To represent and use number bonds and related subtraction facts within 20. • To solve one-step problems that involve addition and subtraction, using concrete objects and pictorial representations, and missing number problems such as $7 = \square - 9$
Assess and review		• To assess the half-term's work.

■ SCHOLASTIC

Medium-term planning Autumn 2

W	Topic	Curriculum objective
1	Counting and number order	• To count to and across 100, forwards and backwards, beginning with 0 or 1, or from any given number. • To count, read and write numbers to 100 in numerals, count in multiples of twos, fives and tens. • To identify and represent numbers using objects and pictorial representations including the number line, and use the language of: equal to, more than, less than (fewer), most, least. • To read and write numbers from 1 to 20 in numerals and words.
2	Place value and comparing quantities and numbers	• When given a number, identify one more and one less. • To identify and represent numbers using objects and pictorial representations including the number line, and use the language of: equal to, more than, less than (fewer), most, least. • To read and write numbers from 1 to 20 in numerals and words.
3	Developing mental strategies for addition	• To read, write and interpret mathematical statements involving addition (+), subtraction (−) and equals (=) signs. • To represent and use number bonds and related subtraction facts within 20. • To solve one-step problems that involve addition and subtraction, using concrete objects and pictorial representations, and missing number problems.
4	Subtraction as difference	• To read, write and interpret mathematical statements involving addition (+), subtraction (−) and equals (=) signs. • To represent and use number bonds and related subtraction facts within 20. • To add and subtract one-digit and two-digit numbers to 20, including zero. • To solve one-step problems that involve addition and subtraction, using concrete objects and pictorial representations, and missing number problems.
5	Measures	• To compare, describe and solve practical problems for: • lengths and heights (long/short, longer/shorter, tall/short, double/half) • mass or weight (heavy/light, heavier than, lighter than) • capacity/volume (full/empty, more than, less than, quarter) • time (quicker, slower, earlier, later). • To recognise and know the value of different denominations of coins and notes.
6	Addition and subtraction using money	• To read, write and interpret mathematical statements involving addition (+), subtraction (−) and equals (=) signs. • To represent and use number bonds and related subtraction facts within 20. • To add and subtract one-digit and two-digit numbers to 20, including zero. • To solve one-step problems that involve addition and subtraction, using concrete objects and pictorial representations, and missing number problems.
Assess and review		• To assess the half-term's work.

Medium-term planning Spring 1

W	Topic	Curriculum objective
1	Counting, reading and writing number patterns	• To count to and across 100, forwards and backwards, beginning with 0 or 1, or from any given number. • To count, read and write numbers to 100 in numerals, count in multiples of twos, fives and tens. • When given a number, identify one more and one less. • To read and write numbers from 1 to 20 in numerals and words.
2	Doubles and near doubles	• To represent and use number bonds and related subtraction facts within 20. • To add and subtract one-digit and two-digit numbers to 20, including zero. • To solve one-step problems that involve addition and subtraction, using concrete objects and pictorial representations, and missing number problems.
3	Grouping and sharing	• To solve one-step problems involving multiplication and division, calculating the answer using concrete objects, pictorial representations and arrays with the support of the teacher.
4	Fractions	• To recognise, find and name a half as one of two equal parts of an object, shape or quantity.

5	Measures, including time	• To sequence events in chronological order using language such as: before and after, next, first, today, yesterday, tomorrow, morning, afternoon and evening.
		• To tell the time to the hour and half past the hour and draw the hands on a clock face to show these times.
		• To measure and begin to record the following:
		  • lengths and heights
		  • mass/weight
		  • capacity and volume
		  • time (hours, minutes, seconds).

6	Addition and subtraction to 15	• To add and subtract one-digit and two-digit numbers to 20, including zero. • To solve one-step problems that involve addition and subtraction, using objects and pictorial representations, and missing number problems.
Assess and review		• To assess the half-term's work.

Medium-term planning Spring 2

W	Topic	Curriculum objective
1	Counting and place value	• To count, read and write numbers to 100 in numerals, count in different multiples including ones, twos, fives and tens. • When given a number, identify one more and one less. • To identify and represent numbers using objects and pictorial representations including the number line, and use the language of: equal to, more than, less than (fewer), most, least.
2	Addition and subtraction beyond totals of 10	• To add and subtract one-digit and two-digit numbers to 20, including zero. • To solve one-step problems that involve addition and subtraction, using concrete objects and pictorial representations, and missing number problems.
3	Grouping and sharing	• To solve one-step problems involving multiplication and division, calculating the answer using concrete objects, pictorial representations and arrays with the support of the teacher.
4	Shape, position and movement	• To recognise and name common 2D and 3D shapes, including: • 2D shapes (rectangles (including squares), circles and triangles) • 3D shapes (cuboids (including cubes), pyramids and spheres). • To describe position, directions and movements, including half, quarter and three-quarter turns.
5	Measuring and time	• To compare, describe and solve practical problems for: • lengths and heights (long/short, longer/shorter, tall/short, double/half) • mass or weight (heavy/light, heavier than, lighter than) • capacity/volume (full/empty, more than, less than, quarter) • time (quicker, slower, earlier, later). • To measure and begin to record the following: • lengths and heights • mass/weight • capacity and volume • time (hours, minutes, seconds). • To sequence events in chronological order using language such as: before and after, next, first, today, yesterday, tomorrow, morning, afternoon and evening.
6	Addition and subtraction totals to 10	• To add and subtract one-digit and two-digit numbers to 20, including zero. • To solve one-step problems that involve addition and subtraction, using concrete objects and pictorial representations, and missing number problems.
Assess and review		• To assess the half-term's work.

Medium-term planning Summer 1

W	Topic	Curriculum objective
1	Addition to totals to 10	• To count to and across 100, forwards and backwards, beginning with 0 or 1, or from any given number. • To count, read and write numbers to 100 in numerals, count in multiples of twos, fives and tens. • To identify and represent numbers using objects and pictorial representations including the number line, and use the language of: equal to, more than, less than (fewer), most, least. • To read and write numbers from 1 to 20 in numerals and words.
2	Addition and subtraction to 20	• To represent and use number bonds and related subtraction facts within 20. • To add and subtract one-digit and two-digit numbers to 20, including zero. • To solve one-step problems that involve addition and subtraction, using concrete objects and pictorial representations, and missing number problems.
3	Fractions	• To recognise, find and name a half as one of two equal parts of an object, shape or quantity. • To recognise, find and name a quarter as one of four equal parts of an object, shape or quantity.
4	Multiplication and division	• To solve one-step problems involving multiplication and division, calculating the answer using concrete objects, pictorial representations and arrays with the support of the teacher.
5	Measuring	• To measure and begin to record the following: • lengths and heights • mass/weight • capacity and volume • time (hours, minutes, seconds).
6	Moving and turning	• To describe position, directions and movements, including half, quarter and three-quarter turns.
Assess and review		• To assess the half-term's work.

Medium-term planning Summer 2

W	Topic	Curriculum objective
1	Number and place value	• When given a number, identify one more and one less. • To identify and represent numbers using objects and pictorial representations including the number line, and use the language of: equal to, more than, less than (fewer), most, least.
2	Addition and subtraction	• To add and subtract one-digit and two-digit numbers to 20, including zero. • To solve one-step problems that involve addition and subtraction, using concrete objects and pictorial representations, and missing number problems.
3	Fractions	• To recognise, find and name a half as one of two equal parts of an object, shape or quantity. • To recognise, find and name a quarter as one of four equal parts of an object, shape or quantity.
4	Multiplication and division	• To solve one-step problems involving multiplication and division, calculating the answer using concrete objects, pictorial representations and arrays with the support of the teacher.
5	Time and using standard units	• To measure and begin to record the following: • lengths and heights • mass/weight • capacity and volume • time (hours, minutes, seconds). • To recognise and use language relating to dates, including days of the week, weeks, months and years. • To tell the time to the hour and half past the hour and draw the hands on a clock face to show these times.
6	Addition to totals to 10	• To order and arrange combinations of objects and shapes in patterns. • To recognise and name common 2D and 3D shapes, including: • 2D shapes (rectangles (including squares), circles and triangles) • 3D shapes (cuboids (including cubes), pyramids and spheres).
Assess and review		• To assess the half-term's work.

Key maths concepts in Year 1

Using practical activities to reinforce concepts of number, place value and calculation

In Year 1, children begin to extend their understanding of number, building on concrete, exploratory approaches used in the Foundation Stage. Practical activities and the physical exploration of concepts continue to play an important part in children's mathematical work in Year 1 and beyond. Children start to use more abstract approaches to mathematical problem solving, including using mathematical statements that involve symbols such as +, − and =.

Working with numbers to 100 and beyond

It can be difficult for young children to grasp larger numbers. They will have learned to work with numbers and groups of objects up to 10, but envisaging numbers greater than this can prove more challenging. Providing children with opportunities to see larger numbers in different contexts will help them to become more familiar with the names and relative values. For example, noticing house numbers as they walk along the street will help them to recognise that number 12 is a long way from number 78. They can also be encouraged to use numbers for practical purposes, such as recording and comparing the numbers of children at school on different days, or comparing the number of paint brushes in a pot to the number of writing pencils, for example.

Place value

By comparing numbers, children will begin to see that it is helpful to look at the first digit in two-digit numbers when comparing numbers for size – for example, 23 is less than 32, because 23 has the first digit 2, whereas 32 has the first digit 3. Using hundred squares and number lines to compare numbers will help children identify the decades that numbers belong to, and so build their understanding of how numbers compare in size. This will help build a firm foundation for the further work on place value which children will undertake in Year 2.

Addition and subtraction

To help children remember the addition and subtraction number bonds to 20, provide them with opportunities to add and subtract in many different contexts, such as dice games, puzzles and differences in race times. Also, use addition and subtraction throughout the school day, for example – *Have we got enough pencils for this group? How many more pencils do we need? Yes, 6 take away 4 is 2. We need two more pencils.*

Year 2 Long-term planning

Number and place value

• Using materials and a range of representations, children should practise counting, reading, writing and comparing numbers to at least 100 and solving a variety of related problems to develop fluency. They should count in multiples of three to support their later understanding of a third.

• As they become more confident with numbers up to 100, children should be introduced to larger numbers to develop further their recognition of patterns within the number system and represent them in different ways, including spatial representations.

• Children should partition numbers in different ways to support subtraction. They become fluent and apply their knowledge of numbers to reason with, discuss and solve problems that emphasise the value of each digit in two-digit numbers. They begin to understand zero as a place holder.

Multiplication and division

• Children should use a variety of language to describe multiplication and division.

• Children should be introduced to the multiplication tables. They practise to become fluent in the 2, 5 and 10 multiplication tables and connect them to each other. They connect the 10 multiplication table to place value, and the 5 multiplication table to the divisions on the clock face. They begin to use other multiplication tables and recall multiplication facts, including using related division facts to perform written and mental calculations.

• Children should work with a range of materials and contexts in which multiplication and division relate to grouping and sharing discrete and continuous quantities, relating these to fractions and measures (e.g. $40 \div 2 = 20$, 20 is a half of 40). They use commutativity and inverse relations to develop multiplicative reasoning (e.g. $4 \times 5 = 20$ and $20 \div 5 = 4$).

Measurement

• Children should use standard units of measurement with increasing accuracy, using their knowledge of the number system. They should use the appropriate language and record using standard abbreviations.

• They should become fluent in telling the time on analogue clocks and recording it.

• Children should also become fluent in counting and recognising coins. They should read and say amounts of money confidently and use the symbols £ and p accurately, recording pounds and pence separately.

Geometry: position and direction

• Children should work with patterns of shapes, including those in different orientations.

• Children should use the concept and language of angles to describe *turn* by applying rotations, including in practical contexts (e.g. children themselves moving in turns, giving instructions to other children to do so, and programming robots using instructions given in right angles).

Fractions

• Children should use additional fractions as 'fractions of' discrete and continuous quantities by solving problems using shapes, objects and quantities. They connect unit fractions to equal sharing and grouping, to numbers when they can be calculated, and to measures, finding fractions of lengths, quantity, a set of objects or shapes. They meet $3/4$ as the first example of a non-unit fraction.

• Children should count in fractions up to 10, starting from any number and using the $1/2$ and $2/4$ equivalence on the number line ($1\frac{1}{4}$, $1\frac{2}{4}$, (or $1\frac{1}{2}$), $1\frac{3}{4}$, 2). This reinforces the concept of fractions as numbers and that they can add up to more than one.

Addition and subtraction

• Children should extend their understanding of the language of addition and subtraction to include sum and difference.

• Children should practise addition and subtraction to 20 to become increasingly fluent in deriving facts such as using $3 + 7 = 10$, $10 - 7 = 3$ and $7 = 10 - 3$ to calculate $30 + 70 = 100$, $100 - 70 = 30$ and $70 = 100 - 30$. They should check their calculations, including by adding to check subtraction and adding numbers in a different order to check addition ($5 + 2 + 1 = 1 + 5 + 2 = 1 + 2 + 5$). This establishes commutativity and associativity of addition.

• Recording addition and subtraction in columns supports place value and prepares for formal written methods with larger numbers.

Geometry: properties of shapes

• Children should handle and name a wider variety of common 2D and 3D shapes and identify the properties of each shape. Children identify, compare and sort shapes on the basis of their properties and use vocabulary precisely, such as sides, edges, vertices and faces.

• Children should read and write names for shapes that are appropriate for their word reading and spelling.

• Children should draw lines and shapes using a straight edge.

Statistics

• Children should record, interpret, collate, organise and compare information (e.g. using many-to-one correspondence with simple ratios 2, 5, 10).

Overview of progression in Year 2

Number and place value

In Year 2, children develop their understanding of place value from Year 1, learning the place value of each digit in a two-digit number; for example, 23 means two tens and three ones. They begin to understand the use of 0 as a place holder. They will build on this when they consider place value in three-digit numbers in Year 3.

Children learn to count in 3s, which will help develop the concept of a third. They order numbers from 0 to 100 and use the <, > and = signs. They become more independent in partitioning numbers in different ways, and this helps to support their work in addition and subtraction.

Addition and subtraction

Children use mental methods to solve problems using addition and subtraction, as well as using objects and pictorial representations. They begin to record addition and subtraction in columns, reinforcing their knowledge of place value. They independently use addition and subtraction facts to 20, and this helps them derive number facts up to 100, such as seeing the parallels between 2 + 6 = 8 and 20 + 60 = 80. They add and subtract different combinations of numbers, including two two-digit numbers. They understand the inverse relationship between addition and subtraction (that one operation undoes the other), and use this to check their calculations.

Multiplication and division

In Year 2, children learn the 2, 5 and 10 multiplication tables, and use these facts in calculations. They recognise that multiplication and division have an inverse relationship, and begin to use the × and ÷ symbols. They learn that multiplication is commutative (2 × 10 is the same as 10 × 2) whereas division is not (10 ÷ 2 is not the same as 2 ÷ 10).

Fractions

Children extend their understanding of fractions to $\frac{1}{3}$ and $\frac{3}{4}$ and learn that $\frac{1}{2}$ is equivalent to $\frac{2}{4}$. They read and write the symbols $\frac{1}{2}$, $\frac{1}{4}$ for example. As well as experimenting practically with fractions and connecting unit fractions to the concepts of sharing and grouping, they begin to write simple fractions, such as $\frac{1}{4}$ of 8 = 2. They will develop this in Year 3 when they learn about tenths and begin to find out more about non-unit fractions.

Measurement

Children learn to independently choose the appropriate standard units for a particular measurement and use a range of different measuring instruments. They recognise and use the £ and p symbols for money (but do not use mixed notation, such as £5.72), and undertake addition and subtraction using money. They learn to tell the time to 5 minutes, including quarter past and quarter to the hour.

Geometry: properties of shapes

By handling common 2D and 3D shapes (including quadrilaterals and cuboids, prisms, cones and polygons) children identify their properties, using the terms *sides, edges, vertices* and *faces*. They compare and sort shapes using their properties.

Geometry: position and direction

Children experiment with making patterns using shapes and begin to use the concept of right angles to describe quarter, half and three-quarter turns. They will develop this concept further in Year 3.

Statistics

Children are introduced to pictograms, tally charts, block diagrams and tables, using these to collate and compare information, and to ask and answer simple questions (for example, finding the number of items in a category, perhaps using one-to-many correspondence, or comparing different categories by quantity).

Medium-term planning Autumn 1

W	Topic	Curriculum objective
1	Number and place value: counting, reading and writing 2-digit numbers, place value	• To count in steps of 2, 3, and 5 from 0, and count in tens from any number, forward or backward. • To recognise the place value of each digit in a two-digit number (tens, ones). • To identify, represent and estimate numbers using different representations, including the number line. • To compare and order numbers from 0 up to 100; use <, > and = signs. • To read and write numbers to at least 100 in numerals and in words. • To use place value and number facts to solve problems.
2	Addition: concrete, visual and number facts	• To solve problems with addition and subtraction: • Using concrete objects and pictorial representations, including those involving numbers, quantities and measures • Applying their increasing knowledge of mental and written methods. • To recall and use addition and subtraction facts to 20 fluently, and derive and use related facts up to 100. • To add and subtract using concrete objects, pictorial representations, and mentally, including: a two-digit number and ones; a two-digit number and tens; two two-digit numbers; adding three one-digit numbers. • To show that addition can be done in any order (commutative) and subtraction cannot. • To recognise and use the inverse relationship between addition and subtraction and use this to check calculations and missing number problems.
3	Subtraction: concrete, visual and number facts	• To solve problems with addition and subtraction: • Using concrete objects and pictorial representations, including those involving numbers, quantities and measures • Applying their increasing knowledge of mental and written methods. • To recall and use addition and subtraction facts to 20 fluently, and derive and use related facts up to 100. • To add and subtract using concrete objects, pictorial representations, and mentally, including: a two-digit number and ones; a 2-digit number and tens; two two-digit numbers; adding three one-digit numbers. • To recognise and use the inverse relationship between addition and subtraction and use this to check calculations and missing number problems.
4	Multiplication and division: repeated addition and repeated subtraction	• To recall and use multiplication and division facts for the 2,5 and 10 multiplication tables, including recognising odd and even numbers. • To calculate mathematical statements for multiplication and division within the multiplication tables and write them using multiplication, division and equals signs. • To recognise and use the inverse relationship between multiplication and division in calculations. • To show that multiplication of two numbers can be done in any order (commutative) and division for one number by another cannot. • To solve problems involving multiplication and division, using materials, arrays, repeated addition, mental methods and multiplication and division facts, including problems in contexts.
5	Geometry: properties of 3D and 2D shape	• To identify and describe the properties of 2D shapes, including the number of sides and symmetry in a vertical line. • To identify and describe the properties of 3D shapes including the number of edges, vertices and faces. • To identify 2D shapes on the surface of 3D shapes, for example circle on a cylinder and a triangle on a pyramid. • To compare and sort common 2D and 3D shapes and everyday objects.
6	Measures: length, mass, capacity, money	• To choose and use appropriate standard units to estimate and measure length/ height in any direction; mass; temperature; volume and capacity to the nearest appropriate unit using rulers, scales, thermometers and measuring vessels. • To compare and order lengths, mass, volume/capacity and record the results using >, < and =. • To recognise and use the symbols for pounds and pence; combine amounts to make a particular value • To find different combinations of coins that equal the same amounts of money • To solve simple problems in a practical context involving addition and subtraction of money of the same unit, including giving change
Assess and review		• To assess the half-term's work.

Medium-term planning Autumn 2

W	Topic	Curriculum objective
1	Number and place value: comparing, ordering two-digit numbers and knowing their place value	• To count in steps of 2, 3, and 5 from 0, and count in tens from any number, forward or backward. • To recognise the place value of each digit in a two-digit number (tens, ones). • To identify, represent and estimate numbers using different representations, including the number line. • To compare and order numbers from 0 up to 100; use <, > and = signs. • To read and write numbers to at least 100 in numerals and in words. • To use place value and number facts to solve problems.
2	Addition and subtraction: using recall of addition and subtraction facts and mental calculation strategies	• To solve problems with addition and subtraction: • Using concrete objects and pictorial representations, including those involving numbers, quantities and measures • Applying their increasing knowledge of mental and written methods. • To add and subtract using concrete objects, pictorial representations, and mentally, including: a two-digit number and ones; a two-digit number and tens; two two-digit numbers; adding three one-digit numbers. • To show that addition can be done in any order (commutative) and subtraction cannot. • To recognise and use the inverse relationship between addition and subtraction and use this to check calculations and missing number problems.
3	Multiplication and division: repeated addition and subtraction, arrays, grouping and using times tables facts	• To recall and use multiplication and division facts for the 2,5 and 10 multiplication tables, including recognising odd and even numbers. • To calculate mathematical statements for multiplication and division within the multiplication tables and write them using the multiplication (×), division (÷) and equals (=) signs. • To recognise and use the inverse relationship between multiplication and division in calculations. • To show that multiplication of two numbers can be done in any order (commutative) and division for one number by another cannot. • To solve one-step problems involving multiplication and division, using materials, arrays, repeated addition, mental methods and multiplication and division facts, including problems in contexts.
4	Fractions: finding fractions of quantities, shapes and sets of objects	• To recognise, find, name and write fractions $\frac{1}{3}$, $\frac{1}{4}$, $\frac{2}{4}$ and $\frac{3}{4}$. • To write simple fractions for example, $\frac{1}{2}$ of 6 = 3 and recognise the equivalence of two quarters and one half.
5	Geometry: position, direction, motion Measures: time	• To order and arrange combinations of mathematical objects in patterns. • To use mathematical vocabulary to describe position, direction and movement, including distinguishing between rotation as a turn and in terms of right angles for quarter, half and three quarter turns (clockwise and anti-clockwise) and movement in a straight line. • To compare and sequence intervals of time. • To tell and write the time to five minutes, including quarter past/to the hour and draw the hands on a clock face to show these times.
6	Data: solving problems that involve collecting data in tallies, tables and pictograms	• To interpret and construct simple pictograms, tally charts, block diagrams and simple tables. • To ask and answer simple questions by counting the number of object in each category and sorting the categories by quantity. • To ask and answer questions about totalling and compare categorical data.
Assess and review		• To assess the half-term's work.

Medium-term planning Spring 1

W	Topic	Curriculum objective
1	Number and place value: estimating, counting and comparing quantities	• To count in steps of 2, 3, and 5 from 0, and count in tens from any number, forward or backward. • To recognise the place value of each digit in a 2-digit number (tens, ones). • To identify, represent and estimate numbers using different representations, including the number line. • To compare and order numbers from 0 up to 100; use <, > and = signs. • To read and write numbers to at least 100 in numerals and in words. • To use place value and number facts to solve problems.
2	Addition and subtraction: using recall of addition and subtraction facts and mental calculation strategies	• To solve problems with addition and subtraction: • Using concrete objects and pictorial representations, including those involving numbers, quantities and measures • Applying their increasing knowledge of mental and written methods. • To recall and use addition and subtraction facts to 20 fluently, and derive and use related facts up to 100. • To add and subtract using concrete objects, pictorial representations, and mentally, including: a two-digit number and ones; a 2-digit number and tens; two 2-digit numbers; adding three one-digit numbers. • To show that addition can be done in any order (commutative) and subtraction cannot. • To recognise and use the inverse relationship between addition and subtraction and use this to check calculations and missing number problems.
3	Addition and subtraction: using partitioning and counting on strategies	• To solve problems with addition and subtraction: • Using concrete objects and pictorial representations, including those involving numbers, quantities and measures • Applying their increasing knowledge of mental and written methods. • To add and subtract using concrete objects, pictorial representations, and mentally, including: a two-digit number and ones; a 2-digit number and tens; two 2-digit numbers; adding three one-digit numbers. • To show that addition can be done in any order (commutative) and subtraction cannot. • To recognise and use the inverse relationship between addition and subtraction and use this to check calculations and missing number problems.
4	Multiplication and division: repeated addition and subtraction, arrays, grouping and using times tables facts	• To recall and use multiplication and division facts for the 2,5 and 10 multiplication tables, including recognising odd and even numbers. • To calculate mathematical statements for multiplication and division within the multiplication tables and write them using the multiplication (×), division (÷) and equals (=) signs. • To recognise and use the inverse relationship between multiplication and division in calculations. • To show that multiplication of two numbers can be done in any order (commutative) and division for one number by another cannot. • To solve problems involving multiplication and division, using materials, arrays, repeated addition, mental methods and multiplication and division facts, including problems in contexts.
5	Geometry: properties of 3D and 2D shape	• To identify and describe the properties of 2D shapes, including the number of sides and symmetry in a vertical line. • To identify and describe the properties of 3D shapes including the number of edges, vertices and faces. • To identify 2D shapes on the surface of 3D shapes, for example circle on a cylinder and a triangle on a pyramid.
6	Measures: length, mass, capacity and money	• To choose and use appropriate standard units to estimate and measure length/height in any direction (m/cm/mm); mass (kg/g); temperature (°C); volume and capacity (litres/ml) to the nearest appropriate unit using rulers, scales, thermometers and measuring vessels. • To compare and order lengths, mass, volume/capacity and record the results using >, < and =.
Assess and review		• To assess the half-term's work.

Medium-term planning Spring 2

W	Title	Curriculum objective
1	Number and place value: estimating, counting, comparing and ordering quantities	• To count in steps of 2, 3, and 5 from 0, and count in tens from any number, forward or backward. • To recognise the place value of each digit in a 2-digit number (tens, ones). • To identify, represent and estimate numbers using different representations, including the number line. • To compare and order numbers from 0 up to 100; use <, > and = signs. • To read and write numbers to at least 100 in numerals and in words. • To use place value and number facts to solve problems.
2	Addition and subtraction: using mental calculation strategies	• To solve problems with addition and subtraction: • Using concrete objects and pictorial representations, including those involving numbers, quantities and measures • Applying their increasing knowledge of mental and written methods. • To recall and use addition and subtraction facts to 20 fluently, and derive and use related facts up to 100. • To add and subtract using concrete objects, pictorial representations, and mentally, including: a two-digit number and ones; a 2-digit number and tens; two 2-digit numbers; adding three one-digit numbers.To show that addition can be done in any order (commutative) and subtraction cannot. • To recognise and use the inverse relationship between addition and subtraction and use this to check calculations and missing number problems.
3	Multiplication and division: repeated addition and subtraction, arrays, grouping and using times tables facts	• To recall and use multiplication and division facts for the 2,5 and 10 multiplication tables, including recognising odd and even numbers. • To calculate mathematical statements for multiplication and division within the multiplication tables and write them using the multiplication (×), division (÷) and equals (=) signs. • To recognise and use the inverse relationship between multiplication and division in calculations. • To show that multiplication of two numbers can be done in any order (commutative) and division for one number by another cannot. • To solve problems involving multiplication and division, using materials, arrays, repeated addition, mental methods and multiplication and division facts, including problems in contexts.
4	Fractions: finding fractions of quantities, shapes and sets of objects	• To recognise, find, name and write fractions $\frac{1}{3}$, $\frac{1}{4}$, $\frac{2}{4}$ and $\frac{3}{4}$. • To write simple fractions for example, $\frac{1}{2}$ of 6 = 3 and recognise the equivalence of two quarters and one half.
5	Geometry: position and direction Measures: time	• To use mathematical vocabulary to describe position, direction and movement, including distinguishing between rotation as a turn and in terms of right angles for quarter, half and three quarter turns (clockwise and anti-clockwise) and movement in a straight line. • To tell and write the time to five minutes, including quarter past/to the hour and draw the hands on a clock face to show these times.
6	Statistics: solving problems that involve collecting data in tallies, tables and pictograms	• To interpret and construct simple pictograms, tally charts, block diagrams and simple tables. • To ask and answer simple questions by counting the number of object in each category and sorting the categories by quantity. • To ask and answer questions about totalling and compare categorical data.
Assess and review		• To assess the half-term's work.

Medium-term planning Summer 1

W	Title	Curriculum objective
1	Number and place value: estimating, counting, comparing and ordering quantities	• To recognise the place value of each digit in a 2-digit number (tens, ones). • To identify, represent and estimate numbers using different representations, including the number line. • To compare and order numbers from 0 up to 100; use <, > and = signs. • To read and write numbers to at least 100 in numerals and in words.
2	Addition and subtraction: using mental calculation strategies	• To solve problems with addition and subtraction: ● Using concrete objects and pictorial representations, including those involving numbers, quantities and measures ● Applying their increasing knowledge of mental and written methods. • To add and subtract using concrete objects, pictorial representations, and mentally, including: a two-digit number and ones; a 2-digit number and tens; two 2-digit numbers; adding three one-digit numbers. • To show that addition can be done in any order (commutative) and subtraction cannot. • To recognise and use the inverse relationship between addition and subtraction and use this to check calculations and missing number problems.
3	Multiplication and division: repeated addition and subtraction, arrays, grouping and using times tables facts	• To recall and use multiplication and division facts for the 2,5 and 10 multiplication tables, including recognising odd and even numbers. • To calculate mathematical statements for multiplication and division within the multiplication tables and write them using the multiplication (×), division (÷) and equals (=) signs. • To recognise and use the inverse relationship between multiplication and division in calculations. • To solve problems involving multiplication and division, using materials, arrays, repeated addition, mental methods and multiplication and division facts, including problems in contexts.
4	Fractions: finding fractions of quantities, shapes and sets of objects	• To recognise, find, name and write fractions $\frac{1}{3}$, $\frac{1}{4}$, $\frac{2}{4}$ and $\frac{3}{4}$. • To write simple fractions for example, $\frac{1}{2}$ of 6 = 3 and recognise the equivalence of two quarters and one half.
5	Geometry: properties of 3D and 2D shape	• To identify and describe the properties of 2D and 3D shapes, including the number of sides, symmetry in a vertical line, edges, vertices, and faces. • To identify 2D shapes on the surface of 3D shapes, for example circle on a cylinder and a triangle on a pyramid. • To compare and sort common 2D and 3D shapes and everyday objects. • To solve one-step problems involving multiplication and division, using materials, arrays, repeated addition, mental methods and multiplication and division facts, including problems in contexts.
6	Measures: length, mass (weight), capacity and money	• To choose and use appropriate standard units to estimate and measure length/height in any direction; mass; temperature; volume and capacity to the nearest appropriate unit using rulers, scales, thermometers and measuring vessels. • To compare and order lengths, mass, volume/capacity and record the results using >, < and =. • To recognise and use symbols for pounds (£) and pence (p); combine amounts to make a particular value. • To find different combinations of coins to equal the same amounts of money • To solve simple problems in a practical context involving addition and subtraction of money of the same unit, including giving change.
Assess and review		• To assess the half-term's work.

Medium-term planning Summer 2

W	Title	Curriculum objective
1	Number and place value: estimating, counting, comparing and ordering quantities	• To recognise the place value of each digit in a 2-digit number (tens, ones). • To identify, represent and estimate numbers using different representations, including the number line. • To compare and order numbers from 0 up to 100; use <, > and = signs. • To read and write numbers to at least 100 in numerals and in words. • To use place value and number facts to solve problems.
2	Addition and subtraction: using partitioning and sequencing	• To solve problems with addition and subtraction: • Using concrete objects and pictorial representations, including those involving numbers, quantities and measures • Applying their increasing knowledge of mental and written methods. • To add and subtract using concrete objects, pictorial representations, and mentally, including: a two-digit number and ones; a 2-digit number and tens; two 2-digit numbers; adding three one-digit numbers. • To recognise and use the inverse relationship between addition and subtraction and use this to check calculations and missing number problems.
3	Fractions: finding fractions of quantities, shapes and sets of objects	• To recall and use multiplication and division facts for the 2,5 and 10 multiplication tables, including recognising odd and even numbers. • To calculate mathematical statements for multiplication and division within the multiplication tables and write them using the multiplication (×), division (÷) and equals (=) signs. • To recognise and use the inverse relationship between multiplication and division in calculations. • To solve problems involving multiplication and division, using materials, arrays, repeate addition, mental methods and multiplication and division facts, including problems in contexts.
4	Finding fractions of quantities, shapes and sets of objects	• To recognise, find, name and write fractions $\frac{1}{3}$, $\frac{1}{4}$, $\frac{2}{4}$ and $\frac{3}{4}$. • To write simple fractions for example, $\frac{1}{2}$ of 6 = 3 and recognise the equivalence of two quarters and one half.
5	Geometry: position and direction Measures: time	• To order and arrange combinations of mathematical objects in patterns. • To use mathematical vocabulary to describe position, direction and movement, including distinguishing between rotation as a turn and in terms of right angles for quarter, half and three quarter turns (clockwise and anti-clockwise) and movement in a straight line. • To compare and sequence intervals of time. • To tell and write the time to five minutes, including quarter past/to the hour and draw the hands on a clock face to show these times.
6	Solving problems by gathering data and representing in tallies, tables, pictograms and block diagrams	• To interpret and construct simple pictograms, tally charts, block diagrams and simple tables. • To ask and answer simple questions by counting the number of objects in each category and sorting the categories by quantity. • To ask and answer questions about totalling and compare categorical data.
Assess and review		• To assess the half-term's work.

Key maths concepts in Year 2

Commutative and non-commutative operations

Commutative operations are those where changing the order of the numbers in the calculation doesn't affect the answer (for example, 2 + 4 = 6, and 4 + 2 = 6). In Year 2, children meet the idea that some mathematical operations are commutative, whereas others are not. It's helpful to give children lots of examples so that they can begin to understand and make this connection for themselves, using objects and pictorial representations as well as written calculations.

Addition and multiplication are commutative:

- 6 + 5 = 11, and 5 + 6 = 11

- 4 × 3 = 12, and 3 × 4 = 12

Children can be encouraged to check that this is true for a wide range of multiplication and addition facts. Using concrete objects such as blocks is a good way to demonstrate that the outcome of addition is always the same , whether you start with for example with 6 blocks and add 5 blocks or vice versa. Similarly, for multiplication, make an array of 4 rows of 3 blocks and then walk around it to see that it is also 3 rows of 4 blocks.

Subtraction and division are non-commutative:

- 5 – 3 does not come to the same as 3 – 5

- 6 ÷ 2 does not come to the same as 2 ÷ 6

As children haven't met negative numbers yet, it isn't necessary to go into detail about the results which give answers in negative numbers – you could say *oh, we haven't got enough to take away five'* or *we'll have to cut the sweets up is we want to divide two sweets between six people*.

Inverse relationships

If two mathematical operations have an inverse relationship, this means that one operation 'undoes' the other (for example, 3 × 6 = 18 can be undone by performing the operation 18 ÷ 6 = 3). This is a concept which children first meet in Year 2, when the idea is introduced that there is an inverse relationship between addition and subtraction, and between multiplication and division.

Children should become familiar with the idea that, for example, you can check the answer to a statement like 2 × 10 = 20 by calculating 20 ÷ 2 = 10, or 20 ÷ 10 = 2. In the same way, you could check 2 + 10 = 12 by calculating 12 – 2 = 10 or 12 – 10 = 2. Plenty of practice is helpful in ensuring that children become fluent in using inverse relationships to check their calculations, and it helps to use concrete objects to demonstrate what is happening visually.

Linking division with fractions

In Year 1, children encountered the idea that division is related to the concept of grouping and sharing quantities (for example, 12 can be divided into 4 groups of 3, or 3 people can share 12 things by getting 4 things each). The idea of sharing can also be used to make a link between division and fractions – so 16 divided (or shared) by 2 is 8, and 8 is half of 16. Again, it will help to use concrete objects to demonstrate this, so children can see that dividing a number of objects by 2 is the same as splitting the group of objects into two halves.

Year 3 Long-term planning

Number and place value

- Children should now be using multiples of 2, 3, 4, 5, 8, 50 and 100.

- Children should use larger numbers to at least 1000, applying partitioning related to place value using varied and increasingly complex problems, building on work in Year 2 (e.g. 146 = 100 and 40 and 6, 46 = 30 and 16).

- Using a variety of representations, including those related to measure, children should continue to count in ones, tens and hundreds, so that they become fluent in the order and place value of numbers to 1000.

Multiplication and division

- Children should continue to practise their mental recall of multiplication tables when they are calculating mathematical statements in order to improve fluency. Through doubling, they connect the 2, 4 and 8 multiplication tables.

- Children should develop efficient mental methods, for example, using commutativity (e.g. $4 \times 12 \times 5 = 4 \times 5 \times 12 = 20 \times 12 = 240$) and multiplication and division facts (e.g. using $3 \times 2 = 6$, $6 \div 3 = 2$ and $2 = 6 \div 3$) to derive related facts ($30 \times 2 = 60$, $60 \div 3 = 20$ and $20 = 60 \div 3$).

- Children should develop reliable written methods for multiplication and division, starting with calculations of two-digit numbers by one-digit numbers and progressing to the formal written methods of short multiplication and division.

- Children should solve simple problems in contexts, deciding which of the four operations to use and why, including measuring and scaling contexts, and correspondence problems in which m objects are connected to n objects (e.g. 3 hats and 4 coats, how many different outfits; 12 sweets shared equally between 4 children; 4 cakes shared equally between 8 children).

Measurement

- Children should continue to measure using the appropriate tools and units, progressing to using a wider range of measures, including comparing and using mixed units (1 kg and 200g) and simple equivalents of mixed units (5m = 500cm).

- The comparison of measures should also include simple scaling and this should connect to multiplication.

- Children should continue to become fluent in recognising the value of coins, by adding and subtracting amounts, including mixed units, and giving change using manageable amounts. They should record £ and p separately. The decimal recording of money is introduced formally in Year 4.

- Children should use both analogue and digital 12-hour clocks and record their times. In this way they become fluent in and prepared for using digital 24-hour clocks in Year 4.

Addition and subtraction

- Children should practise solving varied addition and subtraction questions. For mental calculations with two-digit numbers, the answers could exceed 100.

- Children should use their understanding of place value and partitioning, and practise using columnar addition and subtraction with increasingly large numbers up to three digits to become fluent (see National Curriculum Appendix 1).

Fractions

- Children should connect tenths to place value and decimal measures, not restricted to decimals between 0 and 1 inclusive and to division by 10.

- They should begin to understand unit and non-unit fractions as numbers on the number line, and deduce relations between them, such as size and equivalence. They should go beyond the [0, 1] interval, and $\frac{1}{4} + \frac{3}{4} = 1$ for example, relating this to measure.

- Children should understand the relation between unit fractions as operators and division by integers.

- They should continue to recognise fractions in the context of parts of a whole, numbers, measurements, a shape, or unit fractions as a division of a quantity.

- Children should practise adding and subtracting fractions with the same denominator through a variety of increasingly complex problems to improve fluency.

Geometry: properties of shapes

- Childrens' knowledge of the properties of shapes is extended at this stage to symmetrical and non-symmetrical polygons and polyhedra. Children extend their use of the properties of shapes. They should be able to describe the properties of 2D and 3D shapes using accurate language, including lengths of lines and acute and obtuse for angles greater or lesser than a right angle.

- Children should draw and measure straight lines in centimetres.

Statistics

- Children should understand and use simple scales (e.g. 2, 5, 10 units per cm) in pictograms and bar charts with increasing accuracy.

- They should continue to interpret data presented in many contexts.

Overview of progression in Year 3

Number and place value

In Year 2, children learned about place value in two-digit numbers. In Year 3, they will extend their understanding to include the place value of three-digit numbers – for example, 232 is two hundreds, three tens and two ones. They learn to count in 4s, 8s, 50s and 100s, and work with numbers up to 1000. They begin to use estimation when dealing with number problems involving larger numbers.

Addition and subtraction

In Year 3, children practise mentally adding and subtracting combinations of numbers, including three-digit numbers. When using written methods for addition and subtraction, children learn to write the digits in columns, using their knowledge of place value to align the digits correctly. Children begin to use estimation to work out the rough answer to calculations in advance, and use inverse operations to check their final answers – for example, checking $312 + 43 = 355$ by working out $355 - 43 = 312$.

Multiplication and division

In Year 3, children learn the 3, 4 and 8 multiplication tables, and use their knowledge of doubling to explore links between the 2, 4 and 8 multiplication tables. They use facts from these new multiplication tables to solve multiplication and division problems. Building on their work with written mathematical statements in Year 2, they begin to develop more formal written methods of multiplication and division. They will extend this in Year 4 when they work with more complex multiplication and division problems.

Fractions

Building on work from Year 2, children learn about tenths, and confidently count up and down in tenths. They begin to make links between tenths and place value (ten units make a ten; ten tens make a hundred) and explore connections between tenths and decimal measures. Children extend their understanding of fractions to include more non-unit fractions (that is those with digits other than 1 as their numerator – for example, $\frac{1}{5}$ is a unit fraction, and $\frac{2}{5}$ is a non-unit fraction). They also begin to add and subtract fractions with the same denominator up to one whole, such as $\frac{3}{5} + \frac{3}{5} = \frac{4}{5}$, $\frac{4}{7} - \frac{2}{7} = \frac{2}{7}$.

Measurement

Children will learn to tell the time from analogue 24-hour clocks as well as 12-hour clocks. They will move on to use digital 24-hour clocks in Year 4. They will extend their work on money from Year 2, including working out correct change. They will also learn to measure the perimeter of 2D shapes and solve addition and subtraction problems involving length, mass and volume.

Geometry: properties of shapes

In Year 3, children begin to learn about angle as a property of shapes, and they connect the concept of angles with the idea of turning – for example, realising that two right angles equal a half-turn. They can identify whether a given angle is greater or less than a right angle (obtuse or acute). They can accurately describe lines as horizontal, vertical, perpendicular or parallel.

Statistics

In Year 2, children were introduced to pictograms, tally charts, block diagrams and tables, and this year they use these diagrams to answer an increasing range of questions, including two-step questions (in other words, those where there is a hidden question that needs to be answered before the main question can be tackled) For example, in order to work out *how many more cupcakes did Jon eat than Janie*, children first need to find out how many cakes each person ate.

Medium-term planning Autumn 1

W	Topic	Curriculum objective
1	Reading, writing and ordering two- and three-digit numbers	• To recognise the place value of each digit in a three-digit number (hundreds, tens, ones). • To compare and order numbers up to 1000. • To read and write numbers up to 1000 in numerals and in words.
2	Counting and estimating	• To count from 0 in multiples of 4, 8, 50 and 100; finding 10 or 100 more or less than a given number. • To identify, represent and estimate numbers using different representations.
3	Number facts to 20 and to 100 Addition and Subtraction of 1 and 2-digit numbers	• To add and subtract numbers mentally, including: • a three-digit number and ones • a three-digit number and tens • a three-digit number and hundreds. • To solve problems, including missing number problems, using number facts, place value, and more complex addition and subtraction.
4	Multiplication and division facts	• To recall and use multiplication and division facts for the 3, 4 and 8 multiplication tables. • To write and calculate mathematical statements for multiplication and division using the multiplication tables that they know, including for two-digit numbers times one-digit numbers, using mental and progressing to formal written methods. • To solve problems, including missing number problems, involving multiplication and division, including integer scaling problems and correspondence problems in which *n* objects are connected to *m* objects.
5	Measuring using mm, cm and metres	• To measure, compare, add and subtract: lengths (m/cm/mm); mass (kg/g); volume/capacity (l/ml). • To measure the perimeter of simple 2D shapes.
6	Recognising, describing and making 2D and 3D shapes	• To draw 2D shapes and make 3D shapes using modelling materials; recognise 3D shapes in different orientations and describe them with increasing accuracy. • To identify horizontal, vertical, perpendicular and parallel lines in relation to other lines.
Assess and review		• To assess the half-term's work.

■SCHOLASTIC

Medium-term planning Autumn 2

W	Topic	Curriculum objective
1	Counting and estimating	• To add and subtract numbers mentally, including: • a three-digit number and ones • a three-digit number and tens • a three-digit number and hundreds. • To solve problems, including missing number problems, using number facts, place value, and more complex addition and subtraction.
2	Addition and subtraction of two- and three-digit numbers, using a number line and columns	• To add and subtract numbers with up to three digits, using the efficient written methods of columnar addition and subtraction. • To estimate the answer to a calculation and use inverse operations to check answers. • To solve problems, including missing number problems, using number facts, place value, and more complex addition and subtraction.
3	Multiplication and division: doubling, halving and TU × U	• To recall and use multiplication and division facts for the 3, 4 and 8 multiplication tables. • To write and calculate mathematical statements for multiplication and division using the multiplication tables that they know, including for two-digit numbers times one-digit numbers, using mental and progressing to formal written methods. • To solve problems, including missing number problems, involving multiplication and division, including integer scaling problems and correspondence problems in which n objects are connected to m objects.
4	Fractions: representing, comparing and ordering unit fractions of shapes and numbers	• To recognise, find and write fractions of a discrete set of objects: unit fractions and non-unit fractions with small denominators. • To recognise and use fractions as numbers: unit fractions and non-unit fractions with small denominators. • To compare and order unit fractions, and fractions with the same denominators. • To solve problems that involve all of the above.
5	Read and write time to 5 minute intervals	• To tell and write the time from an analogue clock, including using Roman numerals from I to XII, and 12-hour and 24-hour clocks. • To estimate and read time with increasing accuracy to the nearest minute; record and compare time in terms of seconds, minutes, hours and o'clock; use vocabulary such as am/pm, morning, afternoon, noon and midnight. • To know the number of seconds in a minute and the number of days in each month, year and leap year. • To compare durations of events, for example to calculate the time taken by particular events or tasks.
6	Read, present and interpret pictograms and tables	• To interpret and present data using bar charts, pictograms and tables • To solve one-step and two-step questions such as 'How many more?' and 'How many fewer?' using information presented in scaled bar charts and pictograms and tables.
Assess and review		• To assess the half-term's work.

Medium-term planning Spring 1

W	Topic	Curriculum objective
1	Number, place value and rounding	• To count from 0 in multiples of 4, 8, 50 and 100; finding 10 or 100 more or less than a given number. • To recognise the place value of each digit in a three-digit number (hundreds, tens, ones). • To compare and order numbers up to 1000. • To identify, represent and estimate numbers using different representations. • To read and write numbers up to 1000 in numerals and in words. • To solve number problems and practical problems involving these ideas.
2	Use partitioning to add and subtract two-digit numbers	• To add and subtract numbers mentally, including: • a three-digit number and ones • a three-digit number and tens • a three-digit number and hundreds. • To estimate the answer to a calculation and use inverse operations to check answers. • To solve problems, including missing number problems, using number facts, place value, and more complex addition and subtraction.
3	Multiplication and division: multiplying one-digit numbers by multiples of 10	• To recall and use multiplication and division facts for the 3, 4 and 8 multiplication tables. • To write and calculate mathematical statements for multiplication and division using the multiplication tables that they know, including for two-digit numbers times one-digit numbers, using mental and progressing to formal written methods. • To solve problems, including missing number problems, involving multiplication and division, including integer scaling problems and correspondence problems in which *n* objects are connected to *m* objects.
4	Multiplication and division: practical and informal written methods	• To recall and use multiplication and division facts for the 3, 4 and 8 multiplication tables. • To write and calculate mathematical statements for multiplication and division using the multiplication tables that they know, including for two-digit numbers times one-digit numbers, using mental and progressing to formal written methods. • To solve problems, including missing number problems, involving multiplication and division, including integer scaling problems and correspondence problems in which *n* objects are connected to *m* objects.
5	Measures: adding and subtracting money	• To add and subtract amounts of money to give change, using both £ and p in practical contexts.
6	Recognising and drawing right angles in 2D shapes	• To recognise angles as a property of shape and associate angles with turning. • To identify right angles, recognise that two right angles make a half-turn, three make three quarters of a turn and four a complete turn; identify whether angles are greater than or less than a right angle.
Assess and review		• To assess the half-term's work.

SCHOLASTIC

Medium-term planning Spring 2

W	Topic	Curriculum objective
1	Addition and subtraction of two-digit numbers using columns	• To add and subtract numbers with up to three digits, using the efficient written methods of columnar addition and subtraction. • To estimate the answer to a calculation and use inverse operations to check answers. • To solve problems, including missing number problems, using number facts, place value, and more complex addition and subtraction.
2	Multiplication and division: multiplying by multiples of 10, and dividing with remainders	• To recall and use multiplication and division facts for the 3, 4 and 8 multiplication tables. • To write and calculate mathematical statements for multiplication and division using the multiplication tables that they know, including for two-digit numbers times one-digit numbers, using mental and progressing to formal written methods. • To solve problems, including missing number problems, involving multiplication and division, including integer scaling problems and correspondence problems in which *n* objects are connected to *m* objects.
3	Multiplication and division: multiplying and dividing larger numbers	• To recall and use multiplication and division facts for the 3, 4 and 8 multiplication tables. • To write and calculate mathematical statements for multiplication and division using the multiplication tables that they know, including for two-digit numbers times one-digit numbers, using mental and progressing to formal written methods. • To solve problems, including missing number problems, involving multiplication and division, including integer scaling problems and correspondence problems in which *n* objects are connected to *m* objects.
4	Measuring using grams and kilograms	• To measure, compare, add and subtract: lengths (m/cm/mm); mass (kg/g); volume/capacity (l/ml).
5	Fractions: representing, comparing and ordering unit and non-unit fractions of shapes and numbers	• To count up and down in tenths; recognise that tenths arise from dividing an object into 10 equal parts and in dividing one-digit numbers or quantities by 10. • To recognise, find and write fractions of a discrete set of objects: unit fractions and non-unit fractions with small denominators. • To recognise and use fractions as numbers: unit fractions and non-unit fractions with small denominators. • To recognise and show, using diagrams, equivalent fractions with small denominators. • To compare and order unit fractions, and fractions with the same denominators. • To solve problems that involve all of the above.
6	Read and interpret bar charts, using scales	• To interpret and present data using bar charts, pictograms and tables. • To solve one-step and two-step questions such as 'How many more?' and 'How many fewer?' using information presented in scaled bar charts and pictograms and tables.
Assess and review		• To assess the half-term's work.

Medium-term planning Summer 1

W	Topic	Curriculum objective
1	Read, write and order and round two- and three-digit numbers	• To count from 0 in multiples of 4, 8, 50 and 100; finding 10 or 100 more or less than a given number. • To recognise the place value of each digit in a three-digit number (hundreds, tens, ones). • To compare and order numbers up to 1000. • To identify, represent and estimate numbers using different representations. • To read and write numbers up to 1000 in numerals and in words. • To solve number problems and practical problems involving these ideas.
2	Multiplication and division problems	• To recall and use multiplication and division facts for the 3, 4 and 8 multiplication tables. • To write and calculate mathematical statements for multiplication and division using the multiplication tables that they know, including for two-digit numbers times one-digit numbers, using mental and progressing to formal written methods. • To solve problems, including missing number problems, involving multiplication and division, including integer scaling problems and correspondence problems in which n objects are connected to m objects.
3	Addition and subtraction of three-digit numbers and 1s, 10s and 100s	• To add and subtract numbers mentally, including: • a three-digit number and ones • a three-digit number and tens • a three-digit number and hundreds. • To estimate the answer to a calculation and use inverse operations to check answers. • To solve problems, including missing number problems, using number facts, place value, and more complex addition and subtraction.
4	Addition and subtraction of two- and three-digit numbers using columns	• To add and subtract numbers with up to three digits, using the efficient written methods of columnar addition and subtraction. • To estimate the answer to a calculation and use inverse operations to check answers. • To solve problems, including missing number problems, using number facts, place value, and more complex addition and subtraction.
5	Shape: identifying horizontal, vertical, and curved lines	• To draw 2D shapes and make 3D shapes using modelling materials; recognise 3D shapes in different orientations and describe them with increasing accuracy. • To recognise angles as a property of shape and associate angles with turning. • To identify right angles, recognise that two right angles make a half-turn, three make three quarters of a turn and four a complete turn; identify whether angles are greater than or less than a right angle. • To identify horizontal, vertical, perpendicular and parallel lines in relation to other lines.
6	Measuring using millilitres and litres	• To measure, compare, add and subtract: lengths (m/cm/mm); mass (kg/g); volume/capacity (l/ml).
Assess and review		• To assess the half-term's work.

Medium-term planning Summer 2

W	Topic	Curriculum objective
1	Addition and subtraction of two- and three-digit numbers using and columns	• To add and subtract numbers with up to three digits, using the efficient written methods of columnar addition and subtraction. • To estimate the answer to a calculation and use inverse operations to check answers. • To solve problems, including missing number problems, using number facts, place value, and more complex addition and subtraction.
2	Multiplication and division problems: written methods	• To recall and use multiplication and division facts for the 3, 4 and 8 multiplication tables. • To write and calculate mathematical statements for multiplication and division using the multiplication tables that they know, including for two-digit numbers times one-digit numbers, using mental and progressing to formal written methods. • To solve problems, including missing number problems, involving multiplication and division, including integer scaling problems and correspondence problems in which n objects are connected to m objects.
3	Short multiplication and division	• To recall and use multiplication and division facts for the 3, 4 and 8 multiplication tables. • To write and calculate mathematical statements for multiplication and division using the multiplication tables that they know, including for two-digit numbers times one-digit numbers, using mental and progressing to formal written methods. • To solve problems, including missing number problems, involving multiplication and division, including integer scaling problems and correspondence problems in which n objects are connected to m objects.
4	Fractions: equivalence, addition and subtraction within 1, finding tenths	• To count up and down in tenths; recognise that tenths arise from dividing an object into 10 equal parts and in dividing one-digit numbers or quantities by 10. • To recognise and use fractions as numbers: unit fractions and non-unit fractions with small denominators. • To recognise and show, using diagrams, equivalent fractions with small denominators. • To add and subtract fractions with the same denominator within one whole ($5/7 + 1/7 = 6/7$). • To solve problems that involve all of the above.
5	Read and write time using 12 and 24 hour	• To tell and write the time from an analogue clock, including using Roman numerals from I to XII, and 12-hour and 24-hour clocks. • To estimate and read time with increasing accuracy to the nearest minute; record and compare time in terms of seconds, minutes, hours and o'clock; use vocabulary such as am/pm, morning, afternoon, noon and midnight. • To know the number of seconds in a minute and the number of days in each month, year and leap year. • To compare durations of events, for example to calculate the time taken by particular events or tasks.
6	Construct and interpret bar charts using scales	• To interpret and present data using bar charts, pictograms and tables. • To solve one-step and two-step questions such as 'How many more?' and 'How many fewer?' using information presented in scaled bar charts and pictograms and tables.
Assess and review		• To assess the half-term's work.

Key maths concepts in Year 3

Adding and subtracting fractions with the same denominator within one whole

Children should begin to recognise fractions as numbers that can be used in calculations. Using practical apparatus and examples such as slices of a cake or parts of a sandwich, demonstrate how to add and subtract fractions with the same denominator. Begin with different ways of making one whole by using fractions that have the same denominator, such as a cake that is cut into 8 slices:

$1 = \frac{1}{8} + \frac{7}{8}$ $1 = \frac{5}{8} + \frac{3}{8}$

$1 = \frac{2}{8} + \frac{6}{8}$ $1 = \frac{6}{8} + \frac{2}{8}$

$1 = \frac{3}{8} + \frac{5}{8}$ $1 = \frac{7}{8} + \frac{1}{8}$

$1 = \frac{4}{8} + \frac{4}{8}$

Ask children to explain the pattern in the calculations in the answers. *What stays the same and what changes each time?* (The numerators change but the denominator stays the same.) Emphasise that we're recording how many eighths we have each time. Repeat for other fractions, such as sixths, fifths, tenths, quarters.

In a similar way, discuss subtraction of fractions with the same denominator from one whole:

$1 = \frac{1}{8} + \frac{7}{8}$ $1 = \frac{5}{8} + \frac{3}{8}$

$1 = \frac{2}{8} + \frac{6}{8}$ $1 = \frac{6}{8} + \frac{2}{8}$

$1 = \frac{3}{8} + \frac{5}{8}$ $1 = \frac{7}{8} + \frac{1}{8}$

$1 = \frac{4}{8} + \frac{4}{8}$ $1 - \frac{8}{8} = 0$

Roman numerals from I to XII on clock faces

In Year 2, children will have had practice of telling the time to 5 minutes on analogue clock faces. When introducing Roman numerals on clock faces in Year 3, children can make the link between the number positions that they already know and the new symbols.

The Roman numerals for numbers 1 to 12 are:

1 = I   7 = VII (5 + 2)

2 = II   8 = VIII (5 + 3)

3 = III   9 = IX (10 − 1)

4 = IV (literally, 5 − 1)   10 = X

5 = V   11 = XI (10 + 1)

6 = VI (5 + 1)   12 = XII (10 + 2)

However, many clock faces use IIII for 4. Discuss with children why this might be.

Also, bear in mind that whereas 1, 2, 3 are usually shown upright all around a clock face, Roman numerals tend to be shown with their bases pointing towards the centre of the clock face. This can be confusing for children as the symbols can appear to be reversed. For example, 6 = VI, but is often shown upside down on a clock face as IΛ. You could demonstrate how the numbers radiate out from the centre of the clock face by turning the clock around to show the symbols right way up.

Year 4 Long-term planning

Number and place value

• Using a variety of representations, including measures, children should become fluent in the order and place value of numbers beyond 1000, including counting in tens and hundreds, and maintaining fluency in other multiples through varied and frequent practice.

• They begin to extend their knowledge of the number system to include the decimal numbers and fractions that they have met so far.

• They connect estimation and rounding numbers to the use of measuring instruments.

• Roman numerals should be put in their historical context so children understand that there have been different ways to write whole numbers and that the important concepts of zero and place value were introduced over a period of time.

Addition and subtraction

• Children should continue to practise both mental methods and columnar addition and subtraction with increasingly large numbers to aid fluency (see National Curriculum Appendix 1).

Multiplication and division

• Children should continue to practise recalling and using multiplication tables and related division facts to aid fluency.

• Children should practise mental methods and extend this to three-digit numbers to derive facts, for example $200 \times 3 = 600$ into $600 \div 3 = 200$.

• Children should practise to become fluent in the formal written method of short multiplication for multiplying using multi-digit numbers, and short division with exact answers when dividing by a one-digit number (see Appendix 1).

• Children should write statements about the equality of expressions (e.g. use the distributive law $39 \times 7 = 30 \times 7 + 9 \times 7$ and associative law $(2 \times 3) \times 4 = 2 \times (3 \times 4)$). They combine their knowledge of number facts and rules of arithmetic to solve mental and written calculations, e.g. $2 \times 6 \times 5 = 10 \times 6$.

• Children should solve two-step problems in contexts, choosing the appropriate operation, working with increasingly harder numbers. This should include correspondence questions such as the number of choices of a meal on a menu, or three cakes shared equally between 10 children.

Statistics

• Children should understand and use a greater range of scales in their representations and should begin to relate the graphical representation of data to recording change over time.

Geometry: position and direction

• Children should draw a pair of axes in one quadrant, with equal scales and integer labels. They should read, write and use pairs of coordinates (2, 5), including using coordinate-plotting ICT tools.

Fractions (including decimals)

• Children should connect hundredths to tenths and place value and decimal measure.

• Children should extend the use of the number line to connect fractions, numbers and measures.

• Children should understand the relation between non-unit fractions and multiplication and division of quantities, with particular emphasis on tenths and hundredths.

• Children should make connections between fractions of a length, of a shape and as a representation of one whole or set of quantities. Children should use factors and multiples to recognise equivalent fractions and simplify where appropriate.

• Children should continue practice in adding and subtracting fractions with the same denominator, to become fluent through a variety of increasingly complex problems beyond one whole. Children should be taught throughout that decimals and fractions are different ways of expressing numbers and proportions.

• Children's understanding of the number system and decimal place value should be extended at this stage to tenths and then hundredths. This includes relating the decimal notation to division of whole number by 10 and later 100.

• Children should practise counting using simple fractions and decimal fractions, both forwards and backwards.

• Children should learn decimal notation and the language associated with it, including in the context of measurements. They should make comparisons and order decimal amounts and quantities that are expressed to the same number of decimal places. They should be able to represent numbers with one or two decimal places in several ways, such as on number lines.

Measurement

• Children should build on their understanding of place value and decimal notation to record measures, including money. They should use multiplication to convert from larger to smaller units.

• They should relate area to arrays and multiplication. Perimeter can be expressed algebraically as $2(a + b)$ where a and b are the dimensions in the same unit.

Geometry: properties of shapes

• Children should continue to classify shapes using geometrical properties, extending to classifying different triangles and quadrilaterals.

• Children should compare and order angles in preparation for using a protractor and compare lengths and angles to decide if a polygon is regular or irregular.

• Children should draw symmetric patterns using a variety of media to become familiar with different orientations of lines of symmetry; and recognise line symmetry in a variety of diagrams, including where the line of symmetry does not dissect the reflected shape.

Overview of progression in Year 4

Number and place value

In Year 4, children use place value in four-digit numbers, such as 3742 is three thousands, seven hundreds, four tens and two ones. They learn to count in 6s, 7s, 9s, 25s and 1000s, and say 1000 more or less than a specific number. They encounter negative numbers by counting back past zero on number lines, and continue work on rounding (to the nearest 10, 100 or 1000) and estimation. Children are introduced to Roman numerals to 100 and find out how the number system has changed over time.

Addition and subtraction

Children extend previous years' work by adding and subtracting numbers with up to four digits, using mental and written methods, including columnar addition and subtraction. They keep practising mental methods of addition and subtraction as well as written methods, performing calculations increasingly quickly and confidently. They continue using estimation as well as inverse operations to help check answers.

Multiplication and division

Children learn the remaining multiplication tables up to the 12 multiplication table, and use facts from the tables to solve increasingly complex multiplication and division problems. They build on their work with mental methods of calculation in Year 3, using their knowledge of place value and number facts to multiply and divide confidently. They begin to use a formal written layout for multiplication when multiplying two-digit and three-digit numbers by one-digit numbers.

Fractions (including decimals)

Developing ideas from Year 3, children confidently count up and down in hundredths. They learn about and recognise equivalent fractions, simplifying them when necessary (for example, understanding that $\frac{1}{3} = \frac{2}{6} = \frac{4}{12}$). They move on to understand and show families of equivalent fractions. They build on earlier work, practising adding and subtracting fractions with the same denominator ($\frac{2}{3} + \frac{7}{9} = 1\frac{1}{9}$). Children also work with decimal equivalents of tenths and hundredths and of $\frac{1}{2}$, $\frac{1}{4}$, $\frac{3}{4}$, understanding that decimals and fractions are different ways of expressing numbers. They round numbers with one decimal place to the nearest whole number, and compare numbers with the same number of decimal places, up to two decimal places. They use fractions and decimals to solve straightforward money and measure problems.

Measurement

In Year 3, children learned to measure the perimeter of 2D shapes; they now extend this, calculating the perimeter of rectilinear shapes including squares. They work out the area of rectilinear shapes by counting. Children compare digital clocks and analogue clocks, reading, writing and converting time between the two systems. They begin using £ and p notation to record money.

Geometry: properties of shapes

Children learn about a wider range of geometric shapes, including different types of triangles and quadrilaterals. They develop work on acute and obtuse angles from Year 3, comparing and ordering angles up to two right angles. They work with lines of symmetry in 2D shapes.

Geometry: position and direction

Children begin to work with a coordinate grid (first quadrant only), using coordinates to describe positions on a grid.

Statistics

Children are introduced to the difference between discrete and continuous data, using bar charts for discrete data (numbers of children travelling to school by different methods) and line graphs for continuous data (children's heights). Children will build further on their work with line graphs in Year 5.

Medium-term planning Autumn 1

W	Topic	Curriculum objective
1	Number, place value and rounding	• To recognise the place value of each digit in a four-digit number (thousands, hundreds, tens, and ones). • To identify, represent and estimate numbers using different representations. • To order and compare numbers beyond 1000. • To round any number to the nearest 10, 100 or 1000. • To count in multiples of 6, 7, 9, 25, 1000. • To find 1000 more or less than a given number.
2	Mental addition and subtraction	• To add and subtract numbers with up to four digits using the efficient written methods of columnar addition and subtraction where appropriate. • To solve addition and subtraction two-step problems in contexts, deciding which operations and methods to use and why.
3	Multiplication	• To recall multiplication facts for multiplication tables up to 12 × 12. • To use place value, known and derived facts to multiply and divide mentally, including: multiplying by 0 and 1; dividing by 1; multiplying together three numbers. • To solve problems involving multiplying and adding, including using the distributive law and harder multiplication problems such as which *n* objects are connected to *m* objects.
4	Multiplication and division	• To recall multiplication facts for multiplication tables up to 12 × 12. • To use place value, known and derived facts to multiply and divide mentally, including: multiplying by 0 and 1; dividing by 1; multiplying together three numbers.
5	Geometry: properties of shapes	• To compare and classify geometric shapes, including quadrilaterals and triangles, based on their properties and sizes. • To identify lines of symmetry in 2D shapes presented in different orientations. • To complete a simple symmetric figure with respect to a specific line of symmetry.
6	Measures	• To convert between different units of measure (for example, kilometre to metre; hour to minute). • To measure and calculate the perimeter of a rectilinear figure (including squares) in centimetres and metres. • To solve problems involving converting from hours to minutes; minutes to seconds; years to months; weeks to days. • To estimate, compare and calculate different measures, including money in pounds and pence.
Assess and review		• To assess the half-term's work.

Medium-term planning Autumn 2

W	Topic	Curriculum objective
1	Mental and written addition and subtraction	• To add and subtract numbers with up to four digits using the efficient written methods of columnar addition and subtraction where appropriate. • To estimate and use inverse operations to check answers to a calculation. • To solve addition and subtraction two-step problems in contexts, deciding which operations and methods to use and why.
2	Multiplication	• To recall multiplication facts for multiplication tables up to 12 × 12. • To use place value, known and derived facts to multiply and divide mentally, including: multiplying by 0 and 1; dividing by 1; multiplying together three numbers. • To recognise and use factor pairs and commutativity in mental calculations. • To multiply two-digit and three-digit numbers by a one-digit number using formal written layout. • To solve problems involving multiplying and adding, including using the distributive law and harder multiplication problems such as which n objects are connected to m objects.
3	Multiplication and division	• To recall multiplication facts for multiplication tables up to 12 × 12. • To use place value, known and derived facts to multiply and divide mentally, including: multiplying by 0 and 1; dividing by 1; multiplying together three numbers. • To solve problems involving multiplying and adding, including using the distributive law and harder multiplication problems such as which n objects are connected to m objects.
4	Fractions	• To count up and down in hundredths; recognise that hundredths arise when dividing an object by a hundred and dividing tenths by ten. • To solve problems involving increasingly harder fractions to calculate quantities, and fractions to divide quantities, including non-unit fractions where the answer is a whole number. • To recognise and show, using diagrams, families of common equivalent fractions.
5	Geometry	• To describe positions on a 2D grid as coordinates in the first quadrant. • To plot specified points and draw sides to complete a given polygon. • To compare and classify geometric shapes, including quadrilaterals and triangles, based on their properties and sizes. • To identify acute and obtuse angles and compare and order angles up to two right angles by size.
6	Data handling and time	• To read, write and convert time between analogue and digital 12- and 24-hour clocks. • To solve problems involving converting from hours to minutes; minutes to seconds; years to months; weeks to days. • To interpret and present discrete and continuous data using appropriate graphical methods, including bar charts and time graphs. • To solve comparison, sum and difference problems using information presented in bar charts, pictograms, tables and simple line graphs.
Assess and review		• To assess the half-term's work.

SCHOLASTIC

Medium-term planning Spring 1

W	Topic	Curriculum objective
1	Number, place value and rounding	• To find 1000 more or less than a given number. • To recognise the place value of each digit in a four-digit number (thousands, hundreds, tens, and ones). • To order and compare numbers beyond 1000. • To identify, represent and estimate numbers using different representations. • To round any number to the nearest 10, 100 or 1000. • To solve number and practical problems that involve all of the above and with increasingly large positive numbers. • To read Roman numerals to 100 (I to C) and understand how, over time, the numeral system changed to include the concept of zero and place value.
2	Mental and written addition and subtraction	• To add and subtract numbers with up to four digits using the efficient written methods of columnar addition and subtraction where appropriate. • To estimate and use inverse operations to check answers to a calculation. • To solve addition and subtraction two-step problems in contexts, deciding which operations and methods to use and why. • To estimate, compare and calculate different measures, including money in pounds and pence.
3	Mental and written multiplication	• To recall multiplication and division facts for multiplication tables up to 12 × 12. • To use place value, known and derived facts to multiply and divide mentally, including: multiplying by 0 and 1; dividing by 1; multiplying together three numbers. • To multiply two-digit and three-digit numbers by a one-digit number using formal written layout. • To solve problems involving multiplying and adding, including using the distributive law and harder multiplication problems such as which n objects are connected to m objects.
4	Mental and written division	• To recall multiplication and division facts for multiplication tables up to 12 × 12. • To use place value, known and derived facts to multiply and divide mentally, including: multiplying by 0 and 1; dividing by 1; multiplying together three numbers.
5	Fractions	• To count up and down in hundredths; recognise that hundredths arise when dividing an object by a hundred and dividing tenths by ten. • To solve problems involving increasingly harder fractions to calculate quantities, and fractions to divide quantities, including non-unit fractions where the answer is a whole number. • To recognise and show, using diagrams, families of common equivalent fractions.
6	Fractions and decimals	• To recognise and write decimal equivalents of any number of tenths or hundredths. • To recognise and write decimal equivalents to $\frac{1}{4}$; $\frac{1}{2}$; $\frac{3}{4}$. • To find the effect of dividing a one- or two-digit number by 10 and 100, identifying the value of the digits in the answer as units, tenths and hundredths. • To round decimals with one decimal place to the nearest whole number. • To compare numbers with the same number of decimal places up to two decimal places. • To solve simple measure and money problems involving fractions and decimals to two decimal places.
Assess and review		• To assess the half-term's work.

Medium-term planning Spring 2

W	Topic	Curriculum objective
1	Mental calculation	• To estimate and use inverse operations to check answers to a calculation. • To solve addition and subtraction two-step problems in contexts, deciding which operations and methods to use and why. • To recall multiplication and division facts for multiplication tables up to 12 × 12. • To recognise and use factor pairs and commutativity in mental calculations. • To solve problems involving multiplying and adding, including using the distributive law and harder multiplication problems such as which *n* objects are connected to *m* objects.
2	Written addition and subtraction	• To add and subtract numbers with up to four digits using the efficient written methods of columnar addition and subtraction where appropriate. • To estimate and use inverse operations to check answers to a calculation. • To solve addition and subtraction two-step problems in contexts, deciding which operations and methods to use and why.
3	Time	• To read, write and convert time between analogue and digital 12- and 24-hour clocks. • To solve problems involving converting from hours to minutes; minutes to seconds; years to months; weeks to days.
4	Written multiplication and division	• To recall multiplication and division facts for multiplication tables up to 12 × 12. • To use place value, known and derived facts to multiply and divide mentally, including: multiplying by 0 and 1; dividing by 1; multiplying together three numbers. • To multiply two-digit and three-digit numbers by a one-digit number using formal written layout. • To solve problems involving multiplying and adding, including using the distributive law and harder multiplication problems such as which *n* objects are connected to *m* objects.
5	Geometry	• To compare and classify geometric shapes, including quadrilaterals and triangles, based on their properties and sizes. • To identify acute and obtuse angles and compare and order angles up to two right angles by size. • To describe positions on a 2D grid as coordinates in the first quadrant. • To describe movements between positions as translations of a given unit to the left/right and up/down. • To plot specified points and draw sides to complete a given polygon.
6	Data handling and measurement	• To interpret and present discrete data using bar charts and continuous data using time graphs. • To solve comparison, sum and difference problems using information presented in bar charts, pictograms, tables and simple line graphs. • To convert between different units of measure (kilometre to metre; hour to minute). • To estimate, compare and calculate different measures, including money in pounds and pence.
Assess and review		• To assess the half-term's work.

Medium-term planning Summer 1

W	Topic	Curriculum objective
1	Place value ideas	• To count in multiples of 6, 7, 9, 25 and 1000. • To find 1000 more or less than a given number. • To count backwards through zero to include negative numbers. • To recognise the place value of each digit in a four-digit number (thousands, hundreds, tens, and ones). • To order and compare numbers beyond 1000. • To identify, represent and estimate numbers using different representations. • To round any number to the nearest 10, 100 or 1000. • To solve number and practical problems that involve all of the above and with increasingly large positive numbers.
2	Mental addition and subtraction and measures (use measures as a context for problems)	• To estimate and use inverse operations to check answers to a calculation. • To solve addition and subtraction two-step problems in contexts, deciding which operations and methods to use and why. • To estimate, compare and calculate different measures, including money in pounds and pence.
3	Written addition and subtraction and measures	• To add and subtract numbers with up to four digits using the efficient written methods of columnar addition and subtraction where appropriate. • To estimate and use inverse operations to check answers to a calculation. • To solve addition and subtraction two-step problems in contexts, deciding which operations and methods to use and why.
4	Mental and written multiplication and division	• To recall multiplication and division facts for multiplication tables up to 12 × 12. • To use place value, known and derived facts to multiply and divide mentally, including: multiplying by 0 and 1; dividing by 1; multiplying together three numbers. • To recognise and use factor pairs and commutativity in mental calculations. • To multiply two-digit and three-digit numbers by a one-digit number using formal written layout. • To solve problems involving multiplying and adding, including using the distributive law and harder multiplication problems such as which n objects are connected to m objects.
5	Fractions	• To count up and down in hundredths; recognise that hundredths arise when dividing an object by a hundred and dividing tenths by ten. • To solve problems involving increasingly harder fractions to calculate quantities, and fractions to divide quantities, including non-unit fractions where the answer is a whole number. • To recognise and show, using diagrams, families of common equivalent fractions. • To add and subtract fractions with the same denominator.
6	Area and perimeter of rectilinear shapes and capacity	• To convert between different units of measure (kilometre to metre; hour to minute). • To measure and calculate the perimeter of a rectilinear figure (including squares) in centimetres and metres. • To find the area of rectilinear shapes by counting. • To estimate, compare and calculate different measures, including money in pounds and pence.
Assess and review		• To assess the half-term's work.

Medium-term planning Summer 2

W	Topic	Curriculum objective
1	Mental calculations	• To estimate and use inverse operations to check answers to a calculation. • To solve addition and subtraction two-step problems in contexts, deciding which operations and methods to use and why. • To recall multiplication and division facts for multiplication tables up to 12 × 12. • To recognise and use factor pairs and commutativity in mental calculations. • To solve problems involving multiplying and adding, including using the distributive law and harder multiplication problems such as which *n* objects are connected to *m* objects.
2	Measures	• To convert between different units of measure (kilometre to metre; hour to minute). • To measure and calculate the perimeter of a rectilinear figure (including squares) in centimetres and metres. • To find the area of rectilinear shapes by counting. • To estimate, compare and calculate different measures, including money in pounds and pence. • To read, write and convert time between analogue and digital 12- and 24-hour clocks. • To solve problems involving converting from hours to minutes; minutes to seconds; years to months; weeks to days.
3	Written addition and subtraction	• To add and subtract numbers with up to four digits using the efficient written methods of columnar addition and subtraction where appropriate. • To estimate and use inverse operations to check answers to a calculation. • To solve addition and subtraction two-step problems in contexts, deciding which operations and methods to use and why.
4	Mental and written multiplication and division	• To recall multiplication and division facts for multiplication tables up to 12 × 12. • To use place value, known and derived facts to multiply and divide mentally, including: multiplying by 0 and 1; dividing by 1; multiplying together three numbers. • To recognise and use factor pairs and commutativity in mental calculations. • To multiply two-digit and three-digit numbers by a one-digit number using formal written layout. • To solve problems involving multiplying and adding, including using the distributive law and harder multiplication problems such as which *n* objects are connected to *m* objects.
5	2D shape, angles and coordinates	• To compare and classify geometric shapes, including quadrilaterals and triangles, based on their properties and sizes. • To identify acute and obtuse angles and compare and order angles up to two right angles by size. • To identify lines of symmetry in 2D shapes presented in different orientations. • To describe positions on a 2D grid as coordinates in the first quadrant. • To describe movements between positions as translations of a given unit to the left/right and up/down. • To plot specified points and draw sides to complete a given polygon.
6	Statistics	• To interpret and present discrete and continuous data using appropriate graphical methods, including bar charts and time graphs. • To solve comparison, sum and difference problems using information presented in bar charts, pictograms, tables and simple line graphs.
Assess and review		• To assess the half-term's work.

Key maths concepts in Year 4

Introducing Roman numerals and the history of the number system

In Year 4, children will learn more about Roman numerals (which they first met in Year 3, in the context of analogue clock faces with Roman numerals).

By this stage, children will be familiar with the concept of place value, and the way that our number system allows us to represent any number using only the ten digits 0 to 9. Children will learn that most ancient civilisations (including the Greeks, Romans and Egyptians) used different number systems to ours, which is called the Hindu-Arabic number system.

In the Roman number system, letters were used to represent numbers, with I standing for units, V for fives, X for tens, C for hundreds and M for thousands. Because these letters were repeated to show quantity (such as, III represents 3, XXXVII represents 37 and CCCXXXIII represents 333) many numbers were represented by long and cumbersome chains of letters which are relatively hard to compare and use in written calculations. The Roman system did not include a concept of zero. Our understanding of zero within our current number system was originally developed in India. The Hindu word for zero is 'sunya'.

Children do not need to learn in detail about the different number systems that have prevailed in different times and places throughout history, but it is very helpful for them to get a sense that our current system is a relatively recent development. It's now used throughout the world, however, because of the efficient way it represents larger numbers and can enable us to record mathematical operations efficiently.

Understanding the difference between discrete and continuous data

In Year 3, children met a range of different formats for recording data, including bar charts. They now extend this to include line graphs, and they will need to begin to understand the different circumstances when it is appropriate to use line graphs rather than bar charts. This involves understanding the difference between discrete data (which can be effectively recorded using bar charts) and continuous data (which is more effectively shown on line graphs).

As a rule of thumb, discrete data can be counted, whereas continuous data can be measured. So the number of spots on a ladybird would be discrete data (since ladybirds can only have a whole number of spots) and children could use a bar chart to record the number of spots observed on a group of ladybirds. The chart would clearly show that, for example, 7 ladybirds had five spots, 4 had two spots, 3 had three spots and none had four spots or one spot. Discrete data has units that cannot be split up.

Continuous data is data that can take any value within a range. So, for example, a person could be 152 cm, 152.1 cm, 152.17 cm and so on. Continuous data could be shown on a number line, and every point on the line would have meaning (whereas with discrete data, only certain points have meaning).

Continuous data is shown best on a line graph (or time graph) because it usually shows how a quantity changes over time. For example, children might use a time graph to record how a kitten's weight increased over time, or to record the height of a sunflower plant from seedling to full height.

Year 5 Long-term planning

Number and place value

- Children should identify the place value in large whole numbers.

- They should continue to use number in context, including measurement. Children extend and apply their understanding of the number system to the decimal numbers and fractions they have met so far.

- They should recognise and describe linear number sequences, including those involving fractions and decimals, and find the term-to-term rule.

Multiplication and division

- Children should practise and extend their use of the formal written methods of short multiplication and division (see National Curriculum Appendix 1). They apply all the multiplication tables and related division facts, commit them to memory and use them confidently to make larger calculations.

- They should use and understand the terms factor, multiple and prime, square and cube numbers.

- Children should interpret non-integer answers to division by expressing results in different ways according to the context, including with remainders, as fractions, as decimals or by rounding

- Children use multiplication and division as inverses to support the introduction of ratio in Year 6, by multiplying and dividing by powers of 10 in scale drawings or by multiplying and dividing by powers of a 1000 in converting between units such as kilometres and metres. Distributivity can be expressed as $a(b + c) = ab + ac$ in preparation for using algebra.

Measurement

- Children should use their knowledge of place value and multiplication and division to convert between standard units.

- Children should calculate the perimeter of rectangles and related composite shapes, including using the relations of perimeter or area to find unknown lengths. They calculate the area from scale drawings using given measurements.

- Children should use all four operations in problems involving time and money, including conversions.

Geometry: properties of shapes

- Children should become accurate in drawing lines with a ruler to the nearest millimetre, and measuring with a protractor. They use conventional markings for parallel lines and right angles.

- Children should use the term diagonal and make conjectures about the angles formed by diagonals and sides, and other properties of quadrilaterals, for example using dynamic geometry ICT tools.

- Children should use angle sum facts and other properties to make deductions about missing angles and relate these to missing number problems.

Statistics

- Children should connect their work on coordinates and scales to their interpretation of time graphs.

- They should begin to decide which representations of data are most appropriate and why.

Geometry: position and direction

- Children recognise/use reflection and translation in a variety of diagrams, including continuing to use a 2D grid and coordinates in the first quadrant. Reflection should be in lines parallel to the axes.

Addition and subtraction

- Children should practise using the formal written methods of columnar addition and subtraction with increasingly large numbers to aid fluency.

- They should practise mental calculations with increasingly large numbers to aid fluency.

Fractions (including decimals and percentages)

- Children should be taught throughout that percentages, decimals and fractions are different ways of expressing proportions. They extend their knowledge of fractions to thousandths and connect to decimals and measurres.

- Children should connect equivalent fractions >1 that simplify to integers with division and fractions >1 to division with remainders, using the number line and other models, and hence move from these to improper and mixed fractions.

- Children should connect multiplication by a fraction to using fractions as operators (fractions of), and to division, building on work from previous years. This relates to scaling by simple fractions.

- Children should practise adding and subtracting fractions to become fluent through a variety of increasingly complex problems. They should extend their understanding of adding and subtracting fractions to calculations that exceed 1 as a mixed number.

- Children should read and write proper fractions and mixed numbers accurately and practise counting forwards and backwards in simple fractions.

- Children should continue to develop their understanding of fractions as numbers, measures and operators by finding fractions of numbers and quantities, writing remainders as fractions.

- Children extend counting from Year 4, using decimals and fractions including bridging zero, for example on a number line.

- Children should say, read and write decimal fractions and related tenths, hundredths and thousandths accurately and are confident in checking the reasonableness of their answers to problems.

- They should mentally add and subtract tenths, and one-digit whole numbers and tenths.

- They should practise adding and subtracting decimals including whole numbers and decimals, decimals with different numbers of decimal places, and complements of 1. Children should go beyond the measurement and money models of decimals.

- Children should make connections between percentages, fractions and decimals and relate this to finding 'fractions of'. They recognise that percentages are proportions of quantities as well as operators on quantities.

■ SCHOLASTIC

Overview of progression in Year 5

Number and place value

Children work with numbers up to at least 1,000,000, using knowledge of place value to work out the value of digits. They continue working with negative numbers in different contexts, and practise reading Roman numerals to 1000 (M), which helps them work out years written in Roman numerals. They continue using techniques introduced in earlier years for approximation and estimation.

Addition and subtraction

Children use columns in written addition and subtraction, accurately adding and subtracting numbers with more than four digits. They use mental methods to add and subtract increasingly large numbers, and use rounding to check their answers. With support they choose appropriate operations and methods, and work out the level of accuracy required to answer a particular problem. They will continue to develop this work in Year 6.

Multiplication and division

Children identify multiples and factors, and find all the factor pairs of a given number. With support, they use factors to help solve multiplication and division problems involving larger numbers, and they confidently use written methods to multiply and divide large numbers. They extend their mathematical vocabulary and understanding, beginning to work with prime numbers, prime factors, composite (non-prime) numbers, square and cubed numbers.

Fractions (including decimals and percentages)

Children compare fractions with denominators that are multiples of the same number (comparing $\frac{3}{7}$ with $\frac{6}{14}$). They also identify equivalent fractions of a given fraction including tenths and hundredths. They learn about mixed numbers and improper fractions, and understand how mixed numbers could be converted to improper fractions, and vice versa. With support and using practical equipment and diagrams, they multiply proper fractions and mixed numbers by whole numbers.

Children convert decimal numbers into fractions ($0.65 = \frac{65}{100}$). Extending their work from previous years, they use thousandths and make connections between these and tenths, hundredths and their decimal equivalents. They round decimals to the nearest whole number, and to one decimal place, and begin to work with numbers with three decimal places.

Children begin to work with percentages and find solutions to problems using percentage and decimal equivalents of $\frac{1}{2}$, $\frac{1}{4}$, $\frac{1}{5}$, $\frac{2}{5}$, $\frac{4}{5}$, for example. This forms a basis for further work on percentages in Year 6.

Measurement

In Year 4, children calculated the perimeter of rectilinear shapes; they now extend this to composite (or compound) rectilinear shapes, and calculate the area of squares and rectangles. They begin to understand and estimate volume and capacity, and compare metric with common imperial units. They will build on this work in Year 6.

Geometry: properties of shapes

Children extend their work on angles from Year 4, estimating, measuring, comparing and drawing a variety of angles using degrees. They use given dimensions to help them draw shapes accurately, and use techniques learnt in the context of missing number problems to help them work out missing angles.

Geometry: position and direction

Building on work with coordinate grids from Year 4, children work out the position of shapes following reflection or translation, in the first quadrant.

Statistics

In Year 4, children were introduced to line graphs; now they use information from line graphs to solve problems. They practise completing and reading tables, including timetables.

Medium-term planning Autumn 1

W	Topic	Curriculum objective
1	Place value to 1,000,000	• To read, write, order and compare numbers at least to 1,000,000 and determine the value of each digit. • To count forwards or backwards in steps of powers of 10 for any given number up to 1,000,000.
2	Mental addition and subtraction	• To add and subtract whole numbers with more than 4 digits, including using efficient written methods (columnar addition and subtraction). • To add and subtract numbers mentally with increasingly large numbers. • To solve addition and subtraction multi-step problems in contexts, deciding which operations and methods to use and why.
3	Factors of numbers and prime numbers	• To identify multiples and factors, including finding all factor pairs of a number, and common factors of two numbers. • To multiply and divide whole numbers and those involving decimals by 10, 100 and 1000. • To solve problems involving multiplication and division where larger numbers are used by decomposing them into factors. • To know and use the vocabulary of prime numbers, prime factors and composite (non-prime) numbers. • To establish whether a number up to 100 is prime and recall prime numbers up to 19.
4	Using multiplication and division facts	• To multiply and divide numbers mentally drawing upon known facts. • To multiply and divide whole numbers and those involving decimals by 10, 100 and 1000. • To solve problems involving multiplication and division, including scaling by simple fractions and problems involving simple rates.
5	Angles	• To know angles are measured in degrees; estimate and compare acute, obtuse and reflex angles • To draw given angles, and measure them in degrees ($^{\circ}$). • To identify: • angles at a point and one whole turn (total 360°) • angles at a point on a straight line and ½ a turn (total 180°) • other multiples of 90°.
6	Length, perimeter and area	• To convert between different units of measure (for example, kilometre and metre; metre and centimetre; centimetre and millimetre; kilogram and gram; litre and millilitre). • To understand and use equivalences between metric units and common imperial units such as inches, pounds and pints. • To use all four operations to solve problems involving measure (e.g. length, mass, volume, money) using decimal notation including scaling. • To measure and calculate the perimeter of composite rectilinear shapes in centimetres and metres. • To calculate and compare the area of squares and rectangles including using standard units, square centimetres (cm^2) and square metres (m^2) and estimate the area of irregular shapes.
Assess and review		• To assess the half-term's work.

■SCHOLASTIC

Medium-term planning Autumn 2

W	Topic	Curriculum objective
1	Written methods for multiplication	• To multiply and divide whole numbers and those involving decimals by 10, 100 and 1000. • To multiply numbers up to 4 digits by a one- or two-digit number using an efficient written method, including long multiplication for two-digit numbers. • To solve problems involving multiplication and division, including scaling by simple fractions and problems involving simple rates.
2	Divide 4-digit numbers	• To divide numbers up to 4 digits by a one-digit number using the efficient written method of short division and interpret remainders appropriately for the context. • To multiply and divide numbers mentally drawing upon known facts. • To solve problems involving multiplication and division, including scaling by simple fractions and problems involving simple rates.
3	Fractions and decimals: tenths and hundredths	• To compare and order fractions whose denominators are all multiples of the same number. • To identify, name and write equivalent fractions of a given fraction, represented visually, including tenths and hundredths. • To read and write decimal numbers as fractions (for example, $0.71 = {}^{71}/_{100}$).
4	Decimals: tenths, hundredths, thousandths	• To read, write, order and compare numbers with up to three decimal places. • To read and write decimal numbers as fractions (for example, $0.71 = {}^{71}/_{100}$). • To round decimals with two decimal places to the nearest whole numbers and to one decimal place. • To recognise and use thousandths and relate them to tenths, hundredths and decimals equivalents. • To solve problems involving number up to three decimal places.
5	2D and 3D shapes	• To distinguish between regular and irregular polygons based on reasoning about equal sides and angles. • To use the properties of rectangles to deduce related facts and find missing lengths and angles. • To identify 3D shapes including cubes and cuboids from 2D representations.
6	Tables and bar charts	• To complete, read and interpret information in tables, including timetables.
Assess and review		• To assess the half-term's work.

Medium-term planning Spring 1

W	Topic	Curriculum objective
1	Negative numbers, and solving problems involving numbers	• To read, write, order and compare numbers at least to 1,000,000 and determine the value of each digit. • To count forwards or backwards in steps of powers of 10 for any given number up to 1,000,000. • To interpret negative numbers in context, count forwards and backwards with positive and negative whole numbers through zero. • To round any number up to 1,000,000 to the nearest 10, 100, 1000, 10,000 and 100,000. • To solve number problems and practical problems that involve all of the above.
2	Addition and subtraction of large numbers and money	• To add and subtract whole numbers with more than 4 digits, including using efficient written methods (columnar addition and subtraction). • To add and subtract numbers mentally with increasingly large numbers. • To solve addition and subtraction multi-step problems in contexts, deciding which operations and methods to use and why. • To use rounding to check answers to calculations and determine, in the context of a problem, levels of accuracy. • To solve problems involving numbers up to three decimal places.
3	Long multiplication, square numbers and cube numbers	• To multiply and divide numbers mentally drawing upon known facts. • To multiply and divide whole numbers and those involving decimals by 10, 100 and 1000. • To solve problems involving multiplication and division, including scaling by simple fractions and problems involving simple rates. • To multiply numbers up to 4 digits by a one- or two-digit number using an efficient written method, including long multiplication for two-digit numbers. • To recognise and use square numbers and cube numbers, and the notation for squared (^{2}) and cubed (^{3}). • To calculate and compare the area of squares and rectangles including using standard units, square centimetres (cm^2) and square metres (m^2) and estimate the area of irregular shapes.
4	Adding and subtracting fractions	• To recognise mixed numbers and improper fractions and convert from one form to the other; write mathematical statements > 1 as a mixed number: $\frac{2}{5} + \frac{4}{5} = \frac{6}{5} = \frac{11}{5}$. • To add and subtract fractions with the same denominator and multiples of the same number.
5	Reflections and translations	• To identify, describe and represent the position of a shape following a reflection or translation using the appropriate language, and know that the shape has not changed.
6	Mass	• To convert between different units of measure (kilometre and metre; metre and centimetre; centimetre and millimetre; kilogram and gram; litre and millilitre). • To understand and use basic equivalences between metric units and common imperial units such as inches, pounds and pints. • To use all four operations to solve problems involving measure (e.g. length, mass, volume, money) using decimal notation including scaling.
Assess and review		• To assess the half-term's work.

Medium-term planning Spring 2

W	Topic	Curriculum objective
1	Addition and subtraction: mental and written methods for large numbers	• To add and subtract whole numbers with more than 4 digits, including using efficient written methods (columnar addition and subtraction). • To add and subtract numbers mentally with increasingly large numbers. • To solve addition and subtraction multi-step problems in contexts, deciding which operations and methods to use and why. • To use rounding to check answers to calculations and determine, in the context of a problem, levels of accuracy.
2	Multiplication and division: written methods	• To multiply and divide whole numbers and those involving decimals by 10, 100 and 1000. • To multiply numbers up to 4 digits by a one- or two-digit number using an efficient written method, including long multiplication for two-digit numbers. • To divide numbers up to 4 digits by a one-digit number using the efficient written method of short division and interpret remainders appropriately for the context. • To solve problems involving addition, subtraction, multiplication and division and a combination of these, including understanding the meaning of the equals sign.
3	Calculating with fractions	• To recognise mixed numbers and improper fractions and convert from one form to the other; write mathematical statements > 1 as a mixed number: $\frac{2}{5} + \frac{4}{5} = \frac{6}{5} = 1\frac{1}{5}$. • To add and subtract fractions with the same denominator and multiples of the same number. • To multiply proper fractions and mixed numbers by whole numbers, supported by materials and diagrams.
4	Percentages	• To recognise the per cent symbol (%) and understand that per cent relates to "number of parts per hundred", and write percentages as a fraction with denominator hundred, and as a decimal fraction.
5	Capacity	• To convert between different units of measure (kilometre and metre; metre and centimetre; centimetre and millimetre; kilogram and gram; litre and millilitre). • To understand and use basic equivalences between metric units and common imperial units such as inches, pounds and pints. • To estimate volume and capacity • To use all four operations to solve problems involving measure (e.g. length, mass, volume, money) using decimal notation including scaling
6	Line graphs/ comparative graphs	• To solve comparison, sum and difference problems using information presented in a line graph.
Assess and review		• To assess the half-term's work.

Medium-term planning Summer 1

W	Topic	Curriculum objective
1	Negative numbers and Roman numerals	• To count forwards or backwards in steps of powers of 10 for any given number up to 1,000,000. • To interpret negative numbers in context, count forwards and backwards with positive and negative whole numbers through zero. • To round any number up to 1,000,000 to the nearest 10, 100, 1000, 10,000 and 100,000. • To solve number problems and practical problems that involve all of the above. • To read numerals to 1000 (M) and recognise years written in Roman numerals.
2	Adding and subtracting large and small numbers	• To add and subtract whole numbers with more than 4 digits, including using efficient written methods (columnar addition and subtraction). • To add and subtract numbers mentally with increasingly large numbers. • To solve addition and subtraction multi-step problems in contexts, deciding which operations and methods to use and why. • To use rounding to check answers to calculations and determine, in the context of a problem, levels of accuracy. • To solve problems involving numbers up to three decimal places.
3	Long multiplication and division with remainders	• To multiply numbers up to 4 digits by a one- or two-digit number using an efficient written method, including long multiplication for two-digit numbers. • To divide numbers up to 4 digits by a one-digit number using the efficient written method of short division and interpret remainders appropriately for the context. • To solve problems involving addition, subtraction, multiplication and division and a combination of these, including understanding the meaning of the equals sign.
4	Working with fractions	• To recognise mixed numbers and improper fractions and convert from one form to the other; write mathematical statements > 1 as a mixed number: $\frac{2}{5} + \frac{4}{5} = \frac{6}{5} = \frac{11}{5}$. • To add and subtract fractions with the same denominator and multiples of the same number.

5	Diagonals and problems involving angles	• To know angles are measured in degrees; estimate and compare acute, obtuse and reflex angles
		• To draw given angles, and measure them in degrees ($^{\circ}$).
		• To identify:
		  • angles at a point and one whole turn (total 360°)
		  • angles at a point on a straight line and $\frac{1}{2}$ a turn (total 180°)
		  • other multiples of 90°.
		• To use the properties of a rectangle to deduce related facts and find missing lengths and angles.
		• To distinguish between regular and irregular polygons based on reasoning about equal sides and angles.

6	Volume, time and money	• To estimate volume (e.g. using 1 cm³ blocks to build cubes and cuboids) and capacity (e.g. using water). • To use all four operations to solve problems involving measure (e.g. length, mass, volume, money) using decimal notation including scaling • To solve problems involving converting between units of time.
Assess and review		• To assess the half-term's work.

Medium-term planning Summer 2

W	Topic	Curriculum objective
1	Addition and subtraction of money	• To add and subtract whole numbers with more than 4 digits, including using efficient written methods (columnar addition and subtraction). • To add and subtract numbers mentally with increasingly large numbers. • To solve addition and subtraction multi-step problems in contexts, deciding which operations and methods to use and why.
2	Multiplication and division of money	• To multiply numbers up to 4 digits by a one- or two-digit number using an efficient written method, including long multiplication for two-digit numbers. • To multiply and divide numbers mentally drawing upon known facts. • To identify multiples and factors, including finding all factor pairs of a number, and common factors of two numbers. • To solve problems involving multiplication and division where larger numbers are used by decomposing them into factors. • To solve problems involving addition, subtraction, multiplication and division and a combination of these, including understanding the meaning of the equals sign.
3	Decimals and fractions	• To read, write, order and compare numbers with up to three decimal places. • To read and write decimal numbers as fractions (for example, $0.71 = \frac{71}{100}$). • To recognise and use thousandths and relate them to tenths, hundredths and decimals equivalents. • To round decimals with two decimal places to the nearest whole numbers and to one decimal place.
4	Problems involving percentages	• To recognise the per cent symbol (%) and understand that per cent relates to "number of parts per hundred", and write percentages as a fraction with denominator hundred, and as a decimal fraction. • To solve problems which require knowing percentage and decimal equivalents of $\frac{1}{2}$, $\frac{1}{4}$, $\frac{1}{5}$, $\frac{4}{5}$ and those with a denominator of a multiple of 10 or 25.
5	Perimeter, area and scale drawing	• To measure and calculate the perimeter of composite rectilinear shapes in centimetres and metres. • To calculate and compare the area of squares and rectangles including using standard units, square centimetres (cm^2) and square metres (m^2) and estimate the area of irregular shapes. • To solve problems involving multiplication and division, including scaling by simple fractions and problems involving simple rates.
6	Using tables, and line graphs	• To complete, read and interpret information in tables, including timetables. • To solve comparison, sum and difference problems using information presented in a line graph.
Assess and review		• To assess the half-term's work.

Key maths concepts in Year 5

Introducing negative numbers in context

Children will have encountered negative numbers during Year 4, but in Year 5 they extend their understanding, meeting negative numbers in a range of different contexts.

The idea of negative numbers may seem counterintuitive in some ways – it's clear what we mean by 3 in the context of sweets, jumpers or sheep, but what about –3? Fortunately, there are several everyday contexts which will give children a sense of how useful negative numbers can be. Probably the most familiar context for negative numbers in daily life is temperature. Children will see negative numbers used on a thermometer scale for values below 0°, and they will have heard weather forecasters predicting an overnight drop in temperature, for example to –2°. Children may also be familiar with negative numbers in terms of distances above and below sea level, such as a particular location might be –8 metres (8 metres below sea level). Or they may have used a lift in a large building where the ground floor is marked as 0 on the lift buttons, in which case basement levels may be called –1 and –2.

When introducing negative numbers, it's a good idea to use a vertical number line rather than a horizontal line, because this will help children to use accurate language to describe number relationships above and below zero – for example, they will naturally describe numbers as *falling*, *dropping* or *rising*, and will speak in terms of one number being below or above another. It can be helpful to display the vertical number line like a scale on a giant thermometer.

Refer to numbers less than zero as negative numbers, but allow children to say minus six, minus thirteen, for example.

Comparing percentages with fractions and decimals

Children will need to understand that a percentage is really a fraction with a denominator of 100, so 25% is equivalent to $^{25}/_{100}$. Children will begin to make connections between percentages and decimals when they look at patterns such as this:

15% = 0.15

43% = 0.43

75% = 0.75

The digits are the same, but the decimal point is in a different place. 15% is the same as $^{15}/_{100}$, so drawing on their knowledge of place value, children should begin to understand why the decimal equivalent of 15% is written 0.15.

Percentages below 10% can cause problems because, for example, 5% is not written 0.5 but 0.05 (0.5 being equivalent to $^1/_2$ or 50%). However, place value should also help children avoid giving the wrong decimal equivalent for smaller percentages and fractions.

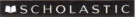

Year 6 Long-term planning

Number and place value

- Children should use the whole number system - saying, reading and writing numbers accurately.

Fractions (including decimals and percentages)

- Children should practise, use and understand the addition and subtraction of fractions with different denominators by identifying equivalent fractions with the same denominator. They should start with fractions where the denominator of one fraction is a multiple of the other and progress to varied and increasingly complex problems.

- Children should use a variety of images to support their understanding of multiplication with fractions. They should use their understanding of the relationship between unit fractions and division to work backwards by multiplying a quantity that represents a unit fraction to find the whole quantity. They practise with simple fractions and decimal fraction equivalents to aid fluency, including listing equivalent fractions to identify fractions with common denominators.

- Children can explore and make conjectures about converting a simple fraction to a decimal fraction. For simple fractions with recurring decimal equivalents, children should learn about rounding the decimal to three decimal places, or other appropriate approximations depending on the context.

- Children are introduced to the division of decimal numbers by one-digit whole numbers and, initially, in practical contexts involving measures and money.

- Children also develop their skills of rounding and estimating as a means of predicting and checking the order of magnitude of their answers to decimal calculations.

Algebra

- Children should be introduced to the use of symbols and letters to represent variables and unknowns in mathematical situations that they already understand, such as:
  - missing numbers, lengths, coordinates and angles
  - formulae in mathematics and science
  - arithmetical rules (e.g. $a + b = b + a$)
  - generalisations of number patterns
  - number puzzles

Geometry: properties of shapes

- Children should draw shapes and nets accurately, using measuring tools and conventional markings and labels for lines and angles.

- Children should describe the properties of shapes and explain how unknown angles and lengths can be derived from known measurements. These relationships might be expressed algebraically.

Geometry: position and direction

- Children should draw and label a pair of axes in all four quadrants with equal scaling.

- Children draw and label rectangles, parallelograms and rhombuses, specified by coordinates in the four quadrants, predicting missing coordinates using the properties of shapes.

Addition, subtraction, multiplication and division

- Children should practise addition, subtraction, multiplication and division for larger numbers, using the efficient written methods of columnar addition and subtraction, short and long multiplication, and short and long division (see Appendix 1).

- They should undertake mental calculations with increasingly large numbers and more complex calculations.

- Children should continue to use all the multiplication tables to calculate mathematical statements in order to maintain their fluency.

- Children should round answers to a specified degree of accuracy.

- Children explore the order of operations using brackets.

- Common factors can be related to finding equivalent fractions.

Ratio and proportion

- Pupils recognise proportionality in contexts when the relations between quantities are in the same ratio.

- Pupils link percentages or 360° to calculatinig angles of pie charts.

- Children should consolidate their understanding of ratio when comparing quantities, sizes and scale drawings by solving a variety of problems. They may use the notation a:b to record their work.

- Children should solve problems involving enequal quantities. These problems are the foundation for later formal approaches to ratio and proportion.

Measurement

- Using the number line, children should use, add and subtract positive and negative integers for measures such as temperature.

- They should know approximate conversions and be able to tell if an answer is sensible.

- They should relate the area of rectangles to parallelograms and triangles, and be able to calculate their areas, understanding and using the formula to do this.

- Children could be introduced to other compound units for speed, such as miles per hour, and apply their knowledge in science or other subjects as appropriate.

Statistics

- Children should connect their work on angles, fractions and percentages to the interpretation of pie charts.

- Children should both encounter and draw graphs relating two variables, arising from their own enquiry and in other subjects.

- They should connect conversion from kilometres to miles in measure to its graphical representation.

- Children should know when it is appropriate to find the mean of a data set.

Overview of progression in Year 6

Number and place value
Children work with numbers up to 10,000,000, using knowledge of place value to work out the value of digits. They continue working with negative numbers in different contexts, and work out intervals across zero.

Addition, subtraction, multiplication and division
Children continue to practise using efficient written and mental methods for all four operations, working with larger numbers and increasingly complex calculations, and confidently using number facts from the multiplication and division tables. They learn about the correct order of operations, understanding that (for example) to work out $(7 + 8) \div 3$ they need to tackle the operation in brackets first.

Fractions (including decimals and percentages)
Children begin to add and subtract fractions with different denominators. They multiply pairs of simple proper fractions together, and divide proper fractions by whole numbers.

Children begin to multiply and divide numbers with two decimal places by one-digit and two-digit whole numbers. They are introduced to this in practical contexts such as measures and money (for example, multiplying 1.80 metres by 2, or dividing £1.80 by 3).

Children extend their work on percentage and decimal equivalents of fractions, begun in Year 5. They work out simple percentages of whole numbers, and encounter equivalences between fractions, decimals and percentages in different contexts.

Ratio and proportion
In Year 6, children are introduced to the concepts of ratio and proportion and use these to compare quantities and sizes; for example, understanding that mixing sugar and flour in a ratio of 1:2 means using 1 part of sugar for every 2 parts of flour, and that the proportion of sugar in the mixture is 1 out of 3 parts, which is $\frac{1}{3}$.

Algebra
Children begin to form an understanding of algebra by encountering the use of symbols and letters to represent unknown elements, for example using letters to represent missing numbers in missing number problems. They also describe and generate number sequences and patterns. They begin to use simple formulae expressed in words, such as 'the perimeter of a rectangle is two times the length plus two times the width.

Measurement
Children extend their Year 5 work on calculating area and estimating volume and capacity to calculate the area of parallelograms and triangles, and work out the volume of cubes and cuboids using standard units. They convert measurements from miles to kilometres.

Geometry: properties of shapes
This year, children make nets to build simple 3D shapes, and work out unknown angles in triangles, quadrilaterals and regular polygons. They draw and name the different parts of a circle (radius, diameter and circumference).

Geometry: position and direction
Extending their work with coordinate grids, children learn to describe positions on all four quadrants of the grid, including using negative numbers. They translate simple shapes on the coordinate plan, reflecting them in the axes.

Statistics
Children continue working with line graphs and also learn how to use pie charts, linking this with their work on angles, percentages and fractions. Children learn how to work out the mean of a set of data and understand when it might be appropriate to calculate the mean, and why.

Medium-term planning Autumn 1

W	Title	Curriculum objective
1	Place value and rounding off	• To read, write, order and compare numbers at least to 10,000,000 and determine the value of each digit. • To round any whole number to a required degree of accuracy. • To solve number problems and practical problems that involve all of the above.
2	Mental and written addition and subtraction of large numbers	• To perform mental calculations, including with mixed operations and large numbers. • To solve addition and subtraction multi-step problems in contexts, deciding which operations and methods to use and why.
3	Multiples, factors and prime numbers	• To perform mental calculations, including with mixed operations and large numbers. • To identify common factors, common multiples and prime numbers. • To solve problems involving addition, subtraction, multiplication and division.
4	Written methods for multiplication and division: HTU × TU and HTU × U	• To multiply multi-digit numbers up to 4 digits by a two-digit whole number using the efficient written method of long multiplication. • To divide numbers up to 4 digits by a two-digit whole number using the efficient written method of long division, and interpret remainders as whole number remainders, fractions or by rounding, as appropriate for the context. • To solve problems involving addition, subtraction, multiplication and division. • To use estimation to check answers to calculations and determine, in the context of a problem, levels of accuracy.
5	Circles and angles	• To illustrate and name parts of circles, including radius, diameter and circumference. • To recognise angles where they meet at a point, are on a straight line, or are vertically opposite, and find missing angles.
6	Units of measure	• To solve problems involving the calculation and conversion of units of measure, using decimal notation to three decimal places where appropriate. • To use, read, write and convert between standard units, converting measurements of length, mass, volume and time from a smaller unit of measure to a larger unit, and vice versa using decimal notation to three decimal places. • To convert between miles and kilometres.
Assess and review		• To assess and review the half-term's work.

Medium-term planning Autumn 2

W	Title	Curriculum objective
1	Written methods for multiplication and division	• To multiply multi-digit numbers up to 4 digits by a two-digit whole number using the efficient written method of long multiplication. • To divide numbers up to 4 digits by a two-digit whole number using efficient written methods of long division and interpret remainders as whole numbers, remainders, fractions or by rounding as appropriate in the context.
2	Comparing, ordering and simplifying fractions	• To compare and order fractions, including fractions >1. • To use common factors to simplify fractions; use common multiples to express fractions in the same denomination.
3	Multiplying decimals by 10, 100 and 1000	• To identify the value of each digit to three decimal places and multiply and divide numbers by 10, 100, 1000 where the answers are up to three decimal places. • To solve problems which require answers to be rounded to specified degrees of accuracy.
4	Order of operations	• To perform mental calculations, including with mixed operations and large numbers. • To use their knowledge of the order of operations to carry out calculations involving the four operations. • To solve addition and subtraction multi-step problems in contexts, deciding which operations and methods to use and why. • To solve problems involving addition, subtraction, multiplication and division. • To use estimation to check answers to calculations and determine, in the context of a problem, levels of accuracy.
5	2D and 3D shapes	• To draw 2D shapes using given dimensions and angles. • To compare and classify geometric shapes based on their properties and sizes and find unknown angles in any triangles, quadrilaterals and regular polygons. • To recognise, describe and build simple 3D shapes, including making nets.
6	Pie charts	• To interpret and construct pie charts and line graphs and use these to solve problems.
Assess and review		• To assess and review the half-term's work.

Medium-term planning Spring 1

W	Title	Curriculum objective
1	Negative numbers, and solving problems involving numbers	• To read, write, order and compare numbers at least to 10,000,000 and determine the value of each digit. • To round any whole number to a required degree of accuracy. • To use negative numbers in context, and calculate intervals across zero. • To solve number problems and practical problems that involve all of the above.
2	Mental and written addition and subtraction of decimals and money	• To perform mental calculations, including with mixed operations and large numbers. • To solve addition and subtraction multi-step problems in contexts, deciding which operations and methods to use and why. • To use estimation to check answers to calculations and determine, in the context of a problem, levels of accuracy.
3	Mental and written multiplication and division	• To perform mental calculations, including with mixed operation and large numbers. • To identify common factors, common multiples and prime numbers (Children could practise using mental methods that involve using factors, for example.) • To use their knowledge of the order of operations to carry out calculations involving the four operations. • To use estimation to check answers to calculations and determine, in the context of a problem, levels of accuracy.
4	Calculating with fractions	• To add and subtract fractions with different denominators, using the concept of equivalent fractions. • To associate a fraction with division to calculate decimal fraction equivalents (0.375) for a simple fraction ($\frac{3}{8}$). • To multiply simple pairs of proper fractions, writing the answer in its simplest form ($\frac{1}{4} \div \frac{1}{2} = \frac{1}{8}$). • To divide proper fractions by whole numbers ($\frac{1}{3} \div 2 = \frac{1}{6}$).
5	Reflections and translations on coordinate axes	• To describe positions on the full co-ordinate grid (all four quadrants). • To draw and translate simple shapes on the co-ordinate plane, and reflect them in the axes.
6	Perimeter, area and volume	• To recognise that shapes with the same area can have different perimeters and vice versa. • To calculate the area of parallelograms and triangles. • To recognise when it is necessary to use the formulae for area and volume of shapes. • To calculate, estimate and compare volume of cubes and cuboids using standard units, including centimetre cubed (cm^3) and cubic metres (m^3) and extending to other units such as mm^3 and km^3.
Assess and review		• To assess and review the half-term's work.

Medium-term planning Spring 2

W	Title	Curriculum objective
1	Calculating with large numbers	• To multiply multi-digit numbers up to 4 digits by a two-digit whole number using the efficient written method of long multiplication. • To divide numbers up to 4 digits by a two-digit whole number using the efficient written method of long division, and interpret remainders as whole number remainders, fractions, or by rounding, as appropriate for the context. • To perform mental calculations, including with mixed operations and large numbers. • To use their knowledge of the order of operations to carry out calculations involving the four operations. • To solve problems involving addition, subtraction, multiplication and division.
2	Multiplying and dividing decimals	• To multiply one-digit numbers with up to two decimal places by whole numbers. • To use written division methods in cases where the answer has up to two decimal places. • To solve problems which require answers to be rounded to specified degrees of accuracy.
3	Percentages, decimals and fractions	• To solve problems involving the calculation of percentages of whole numbers or measures and the use of percentages for comparison. • To recall and use equivalences between simple fractions, decimals and percentages, including different contexts.
4	Simple formulae	• To express missing number problems algebraically. • To use simple formulae expressed in words. • To find pairs of numbers that satisfy number sentences involving two unknowns. • To enumerate all possibilities of combinations of two variables.
5	Area and volume	• To solve problems involving the calculation and conversion of units of measure, using decimal notation to three decimal places, where appropriate. • To use read, write and convert between standard units, converting measurements of length, mass, volume and time from a smaller unit of measure to a larger unit and vice versa, using decimal notation to three decimal places. • To calculate the area of parallelograms and triangles. • To recognise when it is necessary to use the formulae for area and volume of shapes.
6	Line graphs	• To interpret and construct pie charts and line graphs and use these to solve problems.
Assess and review		• To assess and review the half-term's work.

Medium-term planning Summer 1

W	Title	Curriculum objective
1	Problems involving number	• To read, write, order and compare numbers up to 10,000,000 and determine the value of each digit. • To round any whole number to a required degree of accuracy. • To use negative numbers in context and calculate intervals across zero. • To solve number problems and practical problems that involve all the above.
2	Adding and subtracting large and small numbers	• To perform mental calculations, including with mixed operations and large numbers. • To solve addition and subtraction multi-step problems in contexts, deciding which operations to use and why. • To use estimation to check answers to calculations and determine, in the context of a problem, levels of accuracy.
3	Long multiplication and division	• To multiply multi-digit numbers up to 4 digits by a two-digit whole number using the efficient written methods of long multiplication. • To divide numbers up to 4 digits by two digit whole numbers using the efficient written method of long division and interpret remainders as whole number remainders, fractions or by rounding, as appropriate for the context. • To use estimation to check answers to calculations and determine, in the context of a problem, levels of accuracy.
4	Working with fractions	• To add and subtract fractions with different denominators and mixed numbers, using the concept of equivalent fractions. • To multiply simple pairs of proper fractions, writing the answer in its simplest form. • To divide proper fractions by whole numbers.
5	Problems involving percentages, fractions and decimals	• To solve problems involving the calculation of percentages of whole numbers or measures and the use of percentages for comparison. • To recall and use equivalences between simple fractions, decimals and percentages including in different contexts.
6	Ratio and proportion	• To solve problems involving the relative size of two quantities where missing values can be found by using integer multiplication and division facts. • To solve problems involving unequal sharing and grouping using knowledge of fractions and multiples. • To solve problems involving similar shapes where the scale factor is known or can be found.
Assess and review		• To assess and review the half-term's work.

Medium-term planning Summer 2

W	Title	Curriculum objective
1	Solving problems involving money	• To multiply multi-digit numbers up to 4 digits by a two-digit whole number using the efficient written method of long multiplication. • To divide numbers up to 4 digits by a two-digit whole number using the efficient written method of long division, and interpret remainders as whole number remainders, fractions, or by rounding, as appropriate for the context. • To perform mental calculations, including with mixed operations and large numbers. • To use their knowledge of the order of operations to carry out calculations involving the four operations. • To solve addition and subtraction multi-step problems in contexts, deciding which operations and methods to use and why. • To solve problems involving addition, subtraction, multiplication and division. • To use estimation to check answers to calculations and determine, in the context of a problem, levels of accuracy.
2	Number puzzles	• To express missing number problems algebraically. • To use simple formulae expressed in words. • To generate and describe linear number sequences. • To find pairs of numbers that satisfy number sentences involving two unknowns. • To enumerate all possibilities of combinations of two variables.
3	Fractions with different denominators	• To multiply simple pairs of proper fractions, writing the answer in its simplest form ($\frac{1}{4} \div \frac{1}{2} = \frac{1}{8}$). • To use common factors to simplify fractions; use common multiples to express fractions in the same denomination. • To add and subtract fractions with different denominators and mixed numbers using the concept of equivalent fractions.
4	Problems involving percentages and decimals	• To solve problems involving the calculation of percentages of whole numbers or measures such as 15% of 360 and the use of percentages for comparison. • To recall and use equivalences between simple fractions, decimals and percentages, including in different contexts.
5	Problems involving measures	• To solve problems involving the calculation and conversion of units of measure, using decimal notation to three decimal places where appropriate. • To use, read, write and convert between standard units, converting measurements of length, mass, volume and time from a smaller unit of measure to a large unit and vice versa, using decimal notation to three decimal places.
6	Using data	• To interpret and construct pie charts and line graphs and use these to solve problems. • To calculate and interpret the mean as an average.
Assess and review		• To assess and review the half-term's work.

■SCHOLASTIC

Key maths concepts in Year 6

Ratio and proportion: solving problems involving unequal sharing

Children will already know that if they want to work out how to share, for example, 20 sweets equally between two people, they can use straightforward division: they can calculate 20 ÷ 2 = 10. However, what if they need to find out how to share 20 sweets between two people in a ratio of 1:3; in other words, where Person A receives three sweets for every one sweet received by Person B?

Children will need to understand that the ratio 1:3 implies that there are 4 'shares' to be parcelled out between the two people (1 + 3 = 4). If 20 sweets = 4 shares, then each share is worth 5 sweets (20 ÷ 4 = 5), so Person A gets one share, consisting of 5 sweets in total, and lucky Person B gets three shares, consisting of 15 (3 × 5 = 15) sweets in total.

When working with ratios and proportions, children will need to understand the distinction between ratio and proportion. A ratio compares part of the whole with another part of the whole; for instance, shortbread might be made using flour, butter and sugar in a ratio of 4:3:2, with four parts of flour and three parts of sugar for every two parts of butter. However a proportion is used to describe a part of the whole in relation to the whole itself; so in this fictional shortbread, the proportion of butter is 3 out of 9 parts, or one third.

Working out the size of the sectors in pie charts

Children will need to understand that in order to create a pie chart, they first need to work out the fraction of the total that each sector represents. They can then convert this fraction to an angle, and draw sectors with the correctly sized angles.

So, for example, imagine the following data set needs to be represented by a pie chart:

- Number of children travelling to school by car: 15

- Number of children travelling to school by bike: 10

- Number of children walking to school: 5

Children would need first to work out the total number of children in the group (30). They can then work out the fraction of the total which makes up each category – so 'car' accounts for 15 out of the 30 children, or $\frac{1}{2}$ of the total; 'bike' accounts for 10 out of 30, or $\frac{1}{3}$; and 'walk' accounts for 5 out of 30, or $\frac{1}{6}$ of the total.

Children will know that there are 360° in a full turn, and this means they can work out the angle needed for each segment by multiplying the fraction by 360°. (In this example, since the numerator of each fraction is 1, you can just divide 360 by the denominator of each fraction.) This gives the following angles for each segment of the pie:

- car 180°

- bike 120°

- walk 60°

Children can then use these angles to draw the sectors on the pie chart.

Mixed-aged planning: Years 1 and 2

The table below summarises the key concepts for mathematics in Years 1 and 2.

	Year 1	Year 2
Number and place value	• Counting to and across 100, forwards and backwards • Numbers from 1 to 20	• Counting in steps of 2, 3, and 5 from 0, and 10s from any number • 2-digit numbers (10s, 1s)
Addition and subtraction	• Mental methods: 1-digit and 2-digit numbers to 20, including zero	• Mental methods: • 2-digit number and ones • 2-digit numbers and tens • two 2-digit numbers • three 1-digit numbers
Multiplication and division	• Solve simple 1-step problems, using concrete objects, pictorial representations and arrays with teacher support	• 2, 5 and 10 tables • Calculate and write mathematical statements within the 2, 5, and 10 tables, using ×, ÷ and =
Fractions	• A half and a quarter of an object, shape or quantity	• $\frac{1}{3}$, $\frac{1}{4}$, $\frac{2}{4}$ and $\frac{3}{4}$ of a length, shape, set of objects or quantity • Equivalent fractions • Write simple fractions, e.g. $\frac{1}{2}$ of 6 = 3
Measurement	• Compare, describe and solve practical problems length, height, mass/weight, capacity/volume, time • Measure and begin to record measurements • Different denominations of coins and notes • Use language of time • Tell the time to the hour and half past	• Standard units for length, height, mass, temperature, capacity • Recognise and use symbols for £ and p • Add and subtract money, including giving change • Tell and write the time to 5 minutes, including quarter past/to
Geometry	• Common 2D and 3D shapes • Objects and shapes in patterns • Half, quarter and three-quarter turns	• Properties of 2D shapes (including symmetry) and 3D shapes • Objects and shapes in patterns • Half, quarter and three-quarter turns (clockwise and anti-clockwise) and movement in a straight line
Statistics		• Pictograms, tally charts, block diagrams and simple tables

Mixed-aged planning: Years 3 and 4

The table below summarises the key concepts for mathematics in Years 3 and 4.

	Year 3	Year 4
Number, place value and rounding	• Count from 0 in multiples of 4, 8, 50 and 100 • Read, write, order and recognise place value of digits in 3-digit numbers (100s, 10s, 1s)	• Count in multiples of 6, 7, 9, 25 and 1000 • Read, write, order and recognise place value of digits in 4-digit numbers (1000s, 100s, 10s, 1s)

Addition and subtraction	• Mental methods:
	  • 3-digit number and 1s
	  • 3-digit number and 10s
	  • 3-digit number and 100s
	• Written methods: efficient methods for numbers with up to 3 digits
		• Mental methods: for increasingly large numbers
		• Written methods: efficient methods for numbers with up to 4 digit

Multiplication and division	• 2, 3, 4, 5, 8 and 10 tables
	• Mental methods: 2-digit numbers times 1-digit numbers
	• Written methods: 2-digit numbers times 1-digit numbers, progressing to efficient written methods
		• 2, 3, 4, 5, 6, 7, 8, 9, 10, 11, 12 tables
		• Mental methods:
		  • multiplying by 0 and 1
		  • dividing by 1
		  • multiplying together three numbers
		• Efficient methods; multiply 2-digit and 3-digit numbers by a 1-digit number

Fractions, decimals and percentages	• Tenths • Unit fractions and non-unit fractions with small denominators • Fractions as numbers • Equivalent fractions • Add and subtract fractions with the same denominator within one whole	• Hundredths • Equivalent fractions • Add and subtract fractions with the same denominator • Decimal equivalents of tenths and hundredths; decimal equivalents of $\frac{1}{4}$, $\frac{1}{2}$, $\frac{3}{4}$ • Round numbers to 1 decimal point to nearest whole number; compare numbers with the same number of decimal places up to 2 decimal point
Measurement	• Measure, compare, add and subtract lengths, mass, volume/capacity • Perimeter of simple 2D shapes • Add and subtract money, using both £ and p • Tell the time, including Roman numerals from I to XII, and on 12-hour and 24-hour clocks	• Convert between different units of measure • Measure and calculate perimeter of rectilinear shapes • Find area of rectilinear shapes by counting • Convert time between analogue and digital 12- and 24-hour clocks • Convert between units of time
Geometry	• Draw 2D shapes and make 3D shapes • Angles as a property of shape • Right angles; 2 right angles = $\frac{1}{2}$ of a turn; 3 right angles = $\frac{3}{4}$ of a turn; 4 right angles = whole turn • Identify whether angles are greater or less than a right angle • Horizontal, vertical, perpendicular and parallel lines	• Classify quadrilaterals and triangles • Identify acute and obtuse angles • Identify lines of symmetry in 2D shapes • Complete a simple symmetric shape • Coordinate grid (1st quadrant) • Translations
Statistics	• Bar charts, pictograms and tables • Scaled bar charts and pictograms and tables	• Bar charts (for discrete data) and line graphs (continuous data) • Greater range of scales

Mixed-aged planning: Years 5 and 6
The table below summarises the key concepts for mathematics in Years 5 and 6.

	Year 5	Year 6
Number, place value and rounding	• Count in steps of powers of 10 to 10,00,000 • Read, write, order and compare numbers to at least 1,000,000	• Read, write, order and compare numbers up to 10,000,000
Addition and subtraction	• Mental methods: increasingly large numbers, e.g. 12 462 – 2300 = 10,162 • Efficient written methods: whole numbers with more than 4 digits	• Mental methods: increasingly large numbers and more complex calculations • Efficient written methods: larger numbers
Multiplication and division	• 2, 3, 4, 5, 6, 7, 8, 9, 10, 11, 12 tables • Mental methods: whole numbers and those involving decimals by 10, 100 and 1000 • Efficient written methods: multiply up to 4-digit numbers by a 1- or 2-digit number, including long multiplication for 2-digit numbers • Efficient written methods: divide up to 4-digit numbers by a 1-digit number, using short division	• 2, 3, 4, 5, 6, 7, 8, 9, 10, 11, 12 tables • Mental methods: increasingly large numbers and carry out more complex calculations • Efficient written methods: multiply up to 4-digit numbers by a 2-digit whole number, using long multiplication • Efficient written methods: divide up to 4-digit numbers by a 2-digit whole number, using long division
Fractions, decimals and percentages	• Mixed numbers and improper fractions • Add and subtract fractions with the same denominator and related fractions; write mathematical statements > 1 as a mixed number; multiply proper fractions and mixed numbers by whole numbers; decimal equivalents of $1/1000$s, $1/100$s and $1/100$s • Round decimals to 2 dp to nearest whole number and to 1 dp; compare numbers with up to 3 dp • Recognise % symbol; write percentages as a fraction and a decimal; percentage and decimal equivalents of $1/2$, $1/4$, $1/5$, $2/5$, $4/5$ and those with a denominator of a multiple of 10 or 25	• Simplifying fractions; equivalent fractions • Add and subtract fractions with different denominators and mixed numbers; multiply proper fractions, writing answer in simplest form; divide proper fractions by whole numbers • Multiply 1-digit numbers with up to 2 decimal point by whole numbers; use written division methods where answer has up to 2 dp • Calculate percentages of whole numbers or measures, e.g. 15% of 360; equivalents between simple fractions, decimals and percentages
Ratio and proportion		• Solve problems involving: the relative sizes of two quantities, including similarity; unequal sharing and grouping
Algebra		• Express missing number problems algebraically; use simple formulae expressed in words; generate and describe linear number sequences; find pairs of numbers that satisfy number sentences involving two unknowns
Measurement	• Convert between different units of measure; equivalent metric and imperial measures; convert time between units of time • Measure and calculate perimeter of composite rectilinear shapes; calculate area of squares and rectangles • Volume and capacity	• Convert between different units of measure, using decimal notation to 3 dp; convert between miles and kilometres; volume standard units • Shapes with the same perimeter have different areas; calculate area of parallelograms and triangles • Use formulae for area and volume

	Year 5	Year 6
Geometry	• Identify 3D shapes from 2D representations • Measure and draw angles in degrees; identify multiples of 90° angles at a point (total 180° and total 360°) reflex angles • Draw shapes • Properties of a rectangle; regular and irregular polygons • Reflect or translate a shape on a coordinate grid (1st quadrant)	• Build 3D shapes, including making nets; classify shapes • Find unknown angles in triangles, quadrilaterals and regular polygons • Circles: circumference, radius, diameter • Find unknown angles at a point, on a straight line, vertically opposite • Coordinate grid (all four quadrants); translate and reflect shapes on coordinate grid
Statistics	• Line graphs; tables, including timetables	• Pie charts and line graphs; mean as an average

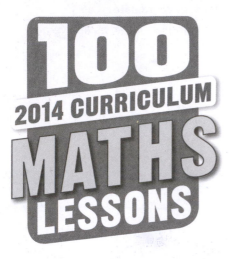
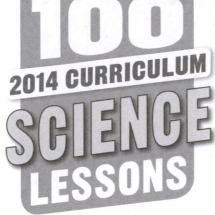
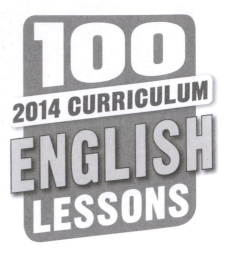